Praise for *A Year of Leading*

A Year of Leading is more than a leadership manual for principals, it's a profound meditation on the essence of leadership itself. Though written for educators, this 40-week guide belongs on the shelf of anyone who aspires to lead people, organizations, or even nations! Kevin captures, with clarity and heart, that the heartbeat of a school is no different from the soul of a society: complex, diverse, emotionally charged, and in need of steady, ethical, and visionary guidance.

>Dr. Gabrielle Serafini, CEO, WelTel Incorporated

This is the kind of leadership book we need right now. Not a checklist. Not a jargon-filled lecture. A guide that meets you where you are—with honesty, humility, and hard-won insight. It doesn't pretend to have all the answers, but it offers the right questions—and the space to sit with them. For leaders who want more than tips and tricks, this book delivers something deeper: meaning, clarity, and purpose.

>Dr. Tsnomot Brad Baker, Superintendent of Indigenous Education,
>BC Ministry of Education and Child Care

A Year of Leading will serve as a compass to guide both aspiring and experienced leaders who seek to serve in a manner that supports the development of communities characterized by belonging, resilience, and commitment to oneself and others. It is, indeed, a mentor-in-print. Weaving together the warp and woof of domains of competency ranging from the visionary to the operational, the book crafts the kind of beautiful whole cloth necessary to enable and sustain inspirational leaders who, in turn, enable and sustain flourishing communities. It is at one and the same time insightful, inspiring, and accessible.

>Paul Neufeld, Ph.D.,
>Associate Professor, Faculty of Education, Simon Fraser University

A Year of Leading is more than just a book; it is a mentor, a compass, and a steady coach guiding you through the complex and unpredictable terrain of school leadership. It offers insights while prompting leaders to engage deeply in reflecting through their own experiences. Leadership is not about simply following a predetermined route—it's about understanding the terrain, embracing challenges, and forging meaningful connections. *A Year of Leading* is a valuable companion for any educator committed to leading with purpose and heart.

> Dr. Andrea McComb, BCPVPA Director of Professional Learning

In *A Year of Leading*, Kevin offers an approachable style that makes complex ideas easy to digest, and his ability to genuinely listen and connect with others shines through every page. Read this book to discover practical strategies that empower you to take charge of your life, cultivate meaningful connections, and reignite your creative spark no matter where you are on your leadership journey.

> Shawn Lockhart, Boundary School District Principal

A Year of Leading really embodies a "career" of leading, learning, and growing. This book should be on the desk of every principal, vice-principal, and school leader in every school district in North America. It is a career's worth of learning and wisdom packed into 300 inspirational pages.

> Geoff Manning, Campbell River School District Superintendent

Kevin Reimer has produced a wonderful, structured guidance handbook for school leaders at the beginning of their career as well as for those who need a refresher. He has utilized his vast skills and knowledge of school leadership in practice, as well as theory, to produce a blended authentic human approach to our profession. In my opinion, school leadership is 70 percent relationships in the 21st century, and Kevin's book exemplifies this. I believe this handbook will have wide appeal internationally as well as nationally in Canada.

> Fiona Forbes, Principal, Peel Language Development School, International Confederation of Principals Past President

A YEAR OF LEADING

A 40-Week Leadership Compass
for Principals and Vice-Principals

KEVIN REIMER

Copyright © 2025 Kevin Reimer

All rights reserved. No part of this publication may be reproduced, distributed, or transmitted in any form or by any means, including photocopying, recording, or other electronic or mechanical methods, without the prior written permission of the publisher, except in the case of brief quotations embodied in critical reviews and certain other noncommercial uses permitted by copyright law.

ISBN 978-1-0695482-0-7 (paperback)
ISBN 978-1-0691591-1-3 (e-book)

Published by:
Illume Leadership
Courtenay, BC, Canada
kevin@howtoprincipal.com

To my wife, Karen, and our children, Owen and Sophie:
Your patience, love, and unwavering support have been the foundation of everything I do. Watching you navigate the world with grace, compassion, and courage is the greatest inspiration I could ever ask for. When I grow up, I want to be just like you. Thank you for teaching me what truly matters.

Table of Contents

Acknowledgments — xiii

Author's Note — xv

Introduction: Putting *A Year of Leading* into practice — 1

Part 1: Authentic Leadership — 13
Leading with self-awareness, integrity, and consistency between values and actions

1. Architects of integrity: Building ethical leadership — 15
   Leading with integrity to build trust

2. Reading the landscape: Aligning maps and terrain — 21
   Developing leadership self-awareness

3. Kintsugi leadership: Embracing the cracks — 27
   Strengthening leadership by embracing vulnerability and imperfection

4. Bending without breaking: The resilient leader — 33
   Balancing demands while maintaining well-being

5. Rest as rhythm: Strategic pauses — 39
   Harnessing rest and reflection to maintain long-term leadership energy

6. Guiding the way: The lighthouse of curiosity — 47
   Using curiosity to foster continuous learning and adaptive leadership

7. The blueprint of leadership: Developing your brand — 53
   Defining your leadership presence

8. Gratitude: The rechargeable energy of leadership — 59
   Sustaining positivity and motivation

Part 2: Visionary Leadership — 65
Setting a clear direction, inspiring others with purpose, and guiding the school toward its preferred future

9. The mirror and the window: Developing a vision — 67
   Seeing beyond immediate challenges to craft a compelling vision

10. Bridging eras: Integrating tradition with modernity — 73
    Honouring past successes while embracing the future

11. Orchestral harmony: Balancing management and vision in school leadership — 79
    Harmonizing strategic vision with the demands of daily operations

12. Ripples of influence: Small actions, big impacts — 87
    Choosing small actions that lead to meaningful impact

13. Horizon leadership: Balancing the good and the bad — 93
    Managing uncertainty while maintaining a long-term perspective

14. The chisel and the mallet: Sculpting a vision — 99
    Refining and shaping leadership vision

Part 3: Relational Leadership — 107
Building trust, fostering collaboration, and nurturing strong, respectful connections within the school community

15. The investment fund: Relationship management — 109
    Building trust through consistent, intentional actions

16. Climbing the peak: The importance of a trusted base camp — 115
    Developing a reliable leadership support network for sustainable success

17. Building bridges: Connecting people, resources, and ideas — 121
Strengthening school culture through intentional collaboration

18. Anchoring assurance: The safety net of trust — 127
Cultivating trust as the foundation for strong relationships

19. Lighting the way: Empowering aspiring leaders — 133
Identifying and nurturing leadership potential within the school community

20. Tuning the strings: Navigating tension — 139
Handling tension constructively

21. Diplomatic relations: The principal as peacekeeper — 145
Fostering school harmony through trust and diplomacy

22. The juggler's skill: Humour and humility — 151
Using humour and approachability to create a positive leadership presence

Part 4: Instructional Leadership — 157
Fostering a learning culture, developing staff members, and driving improvement

23. Strategic leadership: The principal as Chief Learning Officer — 159
Leading with an instructional focus to drive school-wide learning

24. Nurturing collaboration: A thriving school garden — 165
Cultivating a collective approach to teaching and learning

25. Measuring impact: Is the juice worth the squeeze? — 173
Evaluating efforts and initiatives for meaningful impact

26. Tending the fields: The circle of control — 181
Focusing energy where leadership has the greatest impact

27. Effective leadership: Taking the pulse — 189
Using feedback and data to drive leadership growth

Part 5: Operational Leadership — 195
Managing systems effectively, ensuring smooth day-to-day operations, and creating structures that support a thriving school environment

28. Antivirus leadership: Safeguarding school culture — 197
    Proactively addressing negativity to protect a positive school culture

29. The scales of leadership: Moving between hope and hard truths — 205
    Balancing optimism with a grounded, realistic leadership approach

30. Choosing battles wisely: When to step in and when to step back — 213
    Distinguishing between urgent and essential leadership issues

31. Guiding the flow: The power of boundary leadership — 219
    Establishing clear boundaries to maintain effective leadership

32. Seeing clearly, deciding fairly: Principals as judicious leaders — 225
    Making fair and equitable decisions that sustain trust

33. Beyond the fog: Navigating liminal spaces — 231
    Leading confidently during times of uncertainty and transition

34. Riding the rapids: Successfully leading change — 237
    Guiding the school through transformation

Part 6: Equity-Centred Leadership — 245
Actively challenging inequities, amplifying marginalized voices, and creating inclusive environments where every student can thrive

35. Mirror, mirror: Embracing ontological humility — 247
    Recognizing personal biases to lead with self-awareness and equity

36. Navigating the undercurrents: Subversive leadership — 253
    Challenging inequitable structures with strategic, ethical disruption

37. From roots to canopy: Calmness and stability 259
Creating a safe, stable, and inclusive school environment

38. Tectonic shifts: Challenging the status quo 265
Driving systemic change with vision and courage

39. The WAIT principle: Why am I talking? 271
Mastering the art of listening to foster inclusive dialogue

40. Lunar leadership: Gentle influence, powerful impact 277
Leading through quiet influence and strategic action

Conclusion 283

References 285

About the Author 288

Acknowledgments

My deepest gratitude goes to the principals, teachers, students, and parents who have been my greatest educators throughout this journey. Your patience, insight, and collaboration in our shared efforts have profoundly shaped me as a leader. I've learned so much from each of you, and for that, I am forever grateful. Thank you for allowing me to grow alongside you and for the countless ways you've influenced my understanding of what it means to lead. This work has always been, and will always be, for you.

To Jack MacNeill, your steadfast friendship and belief in this project strengthened me when doubt threatened to take over. You have an extraordinary ability to see potential and to provide support in a way that feels both reassuring and inspirational. I am extremely grateful for your presence in my life and your continued support.

To John Morrison, your enthusiasm for this project was infectious. Your thoughtful feedback and cheerleading provided both encouragement and focus. Thank you for believing in this work and encouraging me when I needed it most.

To Ruth Wilson, my amazing editor and guide, your meticulous attention to detail, thoughtful critiques, and unwavering commitment to this project have been invaluable. You brought clarity and cohesion to my ideas, and your expertise elevated this work in ways I could not have imagined.

To Alex Hennig, the designer of this book, you have beautifully captured its spirit through your clean, purposeful design. Your work not only enhances readability but also brings the metaphors and leadership themes to life. Every page benefits from your thoughtful touch and eye for detail.

To the countless role models who have shaped my understanding of leadership, thank you for your guidance, inspiration, and example: Geoff Manning, Gabby Serafini, Kit Krieger, Andrea McComb, and Brent Koot, among many others. Your mentorship, wisdom, and unwavering commitment to school leadership have made a lasting impact on my leadership journey.

To my wife, Karen, an incredibly supportive spouse and a master teacher, your insights brought the teacher's voice and perspective to this project in ways only you could. Thank you for your steadfast belief in me, your invaluable feedback, and your ability to see possibilities even when I doubted them. Your support and partnership have formed the foundation of this work, and I am endlessly grateful for you.

This book is a culmination of so many contributions, lessons, and collaborations, and I am humbled by the collective impact of all who have been involved. Thank you for sharing this journey with me.

Author's Note

This book weaves themes of equity, diversity, inclusion, kindness, and empathy throughout its chapters, recognizing their essential role in leadership. One of the key competencies covered in this book is Equity-Centred Leadership—a reminder that leadership is not just about policies and strategies but is deeply rooted in character and values. Compassion, empathy, and inclusivity are not additions to leadership; they are its foundation.

Inclusivity requires actively recognizing and valuing the diverse backgrounds, perspectives, and needs within a school community. An inclusive leader fosters belonging, respect, and appreciation for all. This begins with self-awareness—examining biases, seeking diverse viewpoints, and creating spaces where every voice is heard. Advocacy for fairness and justice is not a passive stance but an ongoing, intentional commitment.

As an older but no less wise white male author, I acknowledge that my experiences and background shape my perspective. I hope that I have conveyed my insights and reflections in a way that respects and honours the diverse experiences of all readers. If in any part of this book I have inadvertently overlooked or marginalized any perspective, I sincerely apologize, and I invite you to contact me at *kevin@howtoprincipal.com* to share your experience so that I can continue to deepen my learning and broaden my own perspective.

Introduction: Putting *A Year of Leading* into practice

My first principalship was in an elementary school. After spending most of my career at the middle school level, the move to elementary was both exciting and daunting. Early primary students have an infectious energy and curiosity, but their world differs vastly from what I was used to, and I had much to learn.

One day, as I was greeting students at the school entrance, I felt a gentle tug on my pant leg. Looking down, I saw Grace, a kindergarten student with bright, curious eyes and a backpack almost as big as she was.

"Mr. Reimer, what do you do?" she asked, her voice filled with genuine curiosity.

For kindergarten students, their teacher is the first person to guide them through their new school life. They see their teacher read stories, discuss concepts, guide their problem-solving, and provide encouragement. Their teacher's impact is immediate and tangible; students can directly see and feel their teacher's work.

For elementary students, teachers and support staff roles are highly visible. The teacher-librarian who helps students pick out books, the administrative assistant who keeps the school running and tends to their scrapes and bruises, the educational assistants who provide essential support to students with diverse needs, and the playground supervisors who ensure they play safely—all these roles contribute to the daily functioning of the school and are easily recognizable to the students.

However, a principal's most impactful work tends to be more behind the scenes, which can make it challenging for students to understand what a principal does and why it matters. In the eyes of a kindergarten student, the principal might be the person who speaks at assemblies or walks around the school checking in on classrooms, sometimes talking to teachers or meeting with parents. But they don't witness the strategic planning, problem-solving, and countless decisions that shape their learning environment and school culture, nor would they care if they could.

Grace's question caught me off guard. In middle school, students rarely ask such direct and personal questions. They are more concerned with their own social worlds and academic pressures. But Grace, standing before me, looked up with an expression that demanded a simple, straightforward answer.

I knelt to her level, taking a moment to consider how best to respond. I thought about the many roles I played as a principal—the meetings, the planning, the problem-solving, none of which would likely make sense to a five-year-old. "Grace," I began, choosing my words carefully, "I help everyone do their best."

She tilted her head, contemplating my answer before a smile spread across her face. "Oh, okay!" she said brightly, then ran off to her classroom to start her day. I can't say for sure if I fulfilled her curiosity, but it seemed like I had provided a satisfactory answer to her question.

As I stood up and watched her join her classmates, I reflected on my response. It was simple, yet it captured the essence of my role to some degree of satisfaction. And over time, this exchange has been repeated many times. Whenever another student would ask, "Mr. Reimer, what do you do?" I would smile and repeat, "I help everyone do their best." Sometimes, the response seemed to resonate, sometimes not. But in those words, I found a guiding principle for my leadership. My role wasn't just about the administrative tasks or the strategic decisions; it was about recognizing the potential in every school community member and helping to unlock it. That meant ensuring that teachers had what they needed to teach effectively, that students had what they needed to learn and grow, and that the entire school community felt supported and valued. If the intricacies of my role remained unseen, then I hope that the impact was felt in the flourishing of our school.

As I continued my journey as a school principal, Grace's question and my answer stayed with me. They reminded me daily of the simplicity and depth of my mission—a mission that went beyond the day-to-day tasks and touched the heart of what it meant to lead a school: to help everyone do their best.

Leadership in context

Leadership is a journey that a person should never walk alone. In my own journey, I have been privileged to walk alongside some of the most dedicated and passionate leaders in education. In return, this book is my offering of gratitude and support, a companion for *your* leadership journey. It reflects conversations and lessons I've gathered from school leaders across British Columbia, Canada, and around the world, and that shaped my roles as a principal and former BC Principals' and Vice-Principals' President and Executive Director. These roles offered me a unique perspective: a "30,000-foot view" of school leadership, paired with the deeply personal experience of visiting principals in their schools to "breathe their air."

Sitting in my home in the Comox Valley, on the unceded territory of the K'ómoks First Nation, I reflect on the journey that brought me here. This book is the culmination of years spent visiting schools, listening to principals' stories, and learning from their experiences. From Vancouver's urban sprawl to the remote, isolated schools of Haida Gwaii, I was moved by the profound commitment principals bring to their work no matter where they worked. Despite challenges—whether managing large student populations in city schools or navigating the unique demands of small, close-knit communities—each principal I met demonstrated unwavering dedication to their students, staff, and communities. They were—and are—united by a shared purpose: to lead their schools with compassion, vision, and integrity. This book honours their tireless efforts and the lessons they've shared.

I discovered through these experiences that while the context in which principals operate may differ, the core of effective leadership does not; the essence of leadership lies in the ability to connect with people, inspire and support them, and build a culture of trust and mutual respect.

A mentor in print

I am profoundly grateful for the mentors who have guided and shaped my career. From my early days as a beginning teacher to my role as a principal and a provincial leader, mentorship has been a constant, invaluable source of support and inspiration. The lessons I learned from my mentors helped me navigate the complexities of leadership and instilled in me the importance of paying it forward by mentoring others. This book was written with that spirit in mind.

Mentoring is a powerful tool for professional growth and personal fulfillment. It creates a ripple effect, where the benefits extend far beyond the immediate mentor-mentee relationship. By sharing experiences, insights, and encouragement, mentors help others navigate challenges and unlock potential. In turn, they grow as leaders and individuals themselves.

Among the many incredible mentors I've had, none has influenced me more than my junior high basketball coach, Brent Koot. I met Brent when I was just 13 years old—a pivotal time in my life. Adolescence is often marked by a search for identity, and Brent's positive role modelling offered stability and encouragement when I needed it most.

Brent's mentorship had a lasting impact. His example as a coach, teacher, counsellor, and principal became a blueprint for my own career. In 1977, my basketball teammates and I bonded over early-morning practices, shared victories, and the challenges we faced together, and those friendships remain strong to this day. The values Brent instilled—teamwork, perseverance, and mutual respect—have shaped my life and career. Our continued connection reminds me of the lasting impact mentors can have, not just on an individual's professional growth but on their personal relationships and values.

Mentorship is one of the most powerful tools in leadership. A mentor provides more than advice; they offer a safe space for reflection, a sounding board for ideas, and a source of inspiration. Through their guidance, we find the courage to face challenges, the clarity to make tough decisions, and the encouragement to keep growing.

While nothing can replace the unique relationship between a mentor and mentee, *A Year of Leading* is designed to act as a "mentor in print" for current and aspiring school leaders. It aims to offer the guidance, support, and inspiration you'd expect from a trusted mentor.

Each chapter encourages you to think critically, ask important questions, and stretch beyond your comfort zone. Included in each is a space for reflection, a nudge forward, and the tools to help you lead with skill and confidence.

Remember: Leadership isn't just about personal success; it's about mentoring others and passing on the wisdom and support you've received. That's the true power of mentoring: it creates a legacy that shapes not just one leader but an entire community.

The power of metaphors

As an International Coaching Federation–certified leadership coach, I've seen how metaphors can unlock deeper understanding and shift perspectives. In leadership coaching, they simplify complex ideas, helping leaders recognize patterns and connections they might otherwise overlook. For instance, the metaphor of lighting a torch vividly captures leadership development—igniting potential in others, guiding them forward, and consistently inspiring. Each chapter of this book is rooted in a metaphor, offering principals a lens to understand and apply key leadership traits in their daily work.

Metaphors spark creative thinking, shifting perspectives and encouraging leaders to view challenges from new angles. This reflection is vital for personal and professional growth. More than just clarifying ideas, metaphors inspire innovation, bridging the gap between where a leader is now and where they aspire to be.

Direction versus directions

Imagine holding a compass in one hand and a map in the other. A map provides detailed instructions for every turn, while a compass offers something more fundamental: direction. Like a compass, this book doesn't prescribe a fixed route; rather, it offers guidance to help you chart your own path. This distinction—providing direction versus directions—is central to *A Year of Leading*.

Directions imply a rigid, step-by-step process that can limit a leader's ability to adapt. Every school has its own ecosystem with distinct cultures, challenges, and opportunities. What works in one school might fail in another. A one-size-fits-all approach rarely meets a school's specific needs.

Direction, however, offers the flexibility to respond creatively to unique contexts. This book is designed to help you orient your leadership compass, empowering you to trust your judgment, think critically, and craft solutions that reflect your school's strengths and needs. Leaders don't follow a predetermined map; they forge a path that best serves their community.

How *A Year of Leading* is organized

The 40 chapters of *A Year of Leading* are organized into six parts, each exploring a different research-based leadership competency:
- Part 1: Authentic Leadership
- Part 2: Visionary Leadership
- Part 3: Relational Leadership
- Part 4: Instructional Leadership
- Part 5: Operational Leadership
- Part 6: Equity-Centred Leadership

These competencies represent the essential areas of growth and action required for principals and vice-principals to excel as school leaders, addressing the diverse challenges they face while fostering personal and professional success.
- **Authentic Leadership** emphasizes the inner work of self-awareness, resilience, and personal growth. Research shows that self-aware leaders

inspire trust and build credibility within their communities, enabling them to lead with integrity and adaptability.
- **Visionary Leadership** focuses on crafting and communicating a shared vision that inspires action. Effective leaders motivate their communities by articulating clear goals and aligning their decisions with long-term aspirations, fostering a sense of direction and purpose in their schools.
- **Relational Leadership** highlights the importance of building trust, fostering collaboration, and cultivating meaningful relationships. Strong interpersonal connections are foundational to a thriving school culture, and research consistently underscores the role of relational trust in achieving sustainable change and staff engagement.
- **Instructional Leadership** positions principals as leaders of learning. By guiding teaching and learning practices, promoting professional growth, and centring decisions on student outcomes, instructional leaders ensure student success while supporting teacher efficacy.
- **Operational Leadership** addresses the systems, processes, and decisions that keep schools running smoothly. Leaders who excel in this competency manage resources effectively, make ethical decisions, and create a stable foundation for their school communities to flourish.
- **Equity-Centred Leadership** reflects the moral imperative for leaders to actively promote inclusivity, fairness, and culturally responsive practices. By dismantling systemic barriers and creating equitable opportunities, principals can foster environments in which all students and staff feel valued and supported.

While each of these competencies is vital, effective school leadership is not merely about excelling in one area—it involves balancing and integrating them all. A principal who is visionary but lacks strong relationships may find it challenging to realize their vision. A leader who is highly operational yet detached from instructional leadership can maintain stability but might not drive meaningful learning outcomes. Similarly, equity cannot be an afterthought; it must be embedded in all aspects of leadership, shaping decisions at every level.

Leadership is a dynamic practice that requires principals to adapt to use competencies based on the evolving needs of their school communities. The capability to navigate these domains flexibly—without losing perspective on the larger picture—is what sets exceptional school leaders apart.

How to use this book

There's no right or wrong way to use this book. *A Year of Leading* is designed to meet you wherever you are on your leadership journey. The 40 chapters reflect a typical 40-week school year, but you don't need to follow a linear path. Leadership isn't one-size-fits-all; your engagement with this book can be as flexible as you need.

Every chapter begins by anchoring in a central metaphor or theme that illustrates the leadership concept. These metaphors serve as chapter entry points, making abstract ideas tangible and relatable. By framing leadership traits through vivid imagery, the book invites you to think deeply about your roles and responsibilities.

Each chapter then transitions into practical examples of what the leadership trait looks like in action. The focus is on demonstrating how effective leadership manifests in concrete ways, helping you visualize how you can incorporate these traits into your own school.

Because no leadership approach is without its challenges, each chapter also examines potential blind spots. These are the pitfalls and unintended consequences that can arise when implementing specific leadership strategies. By addressing these challenges openly, the book equips you to anticipate obstacles and adjust your approaches thoughtfully.

Every chapter concludes with reflective open-ended questions that invite you to consider how the leadership trait applies to your own circumstances, offering a space for personal and professional growth. Reflection transforms the content from passive learning into an active tool for self-assessment, and it will help to identify areas for improvement and align your actions with the school's vision and goals.

You can dip into the chapters as situations arise, revisit key ideas when you need fresh perspectives, and engage with the content in a way that mirrors the real-life, evolving nature of mentoring conversations. Some weeks, you might focus on a chapter that directly addresses a challenge or skill you want to develop. Other times, you might skim a chapter for reassurance that you're on the right track. Both approaches are equally valuable. This book is here to support you—whether you're reflecting deeply or seeking quick validation.

You can return to this book whenever your leadership evolves or new challenges arise. Whether you read it weekly, share it in a book club, or refer to it sporadically for a fresh perspective, you're doing it right—because you're doing it your way.

Principals, vice-principals, and school leaders

Throughout this book, I often use the term "principal" to describe school leaders. This choice is intentional, but it is not meant to overlook the vital contributions of vice-principals. Having served as a vice-principal for many years myself, I deeply respect the unique challenges and opportunities of the role. It was during that time that I learned some of my most important leadership lessons from the principals who mentored and challenged me, shaping the leader I would become.

Using "principal" as a catch-all term simplifies the language and ensures clarity, especially for those new to these concepts. When I say "principal," I'm referring to anyone in a formal school leadership position—whether you are a seasoned principal, a vice-principal learning the ropes, or an aspiring leader, the insights in this book are for you.

You'll also see the term "school leader" used throughout the book. This broader term captures the collective contributions of principals, vice-principals, and others in leadership roles. Whether shaping a school's vision or managing its day-to-day operations, your role is integral to your school community. Whatever your title, you play a meaningful part in the journey of your school's community.

A message from the department of redundancy department

One common thread connects all the chapters in this book: essential leadership elements such as transparent communication, empathy, strategic thinking, and active listening.

Leadership is complex, but certain core principles apply universally. Whether navigating a crisis, building a vision, addressing staff challenges, or engaging with the community, foundational practices like effective communication and strategic planning are indispensable. These recurring themes are emphasized intentionally to highlight their importance in effective leadership. In other words, the repetition here is not redundant but deliberate. Revisiting these concepts reinforces understanding, helping you internalize and apply them intuitively. Recognizing their versatility allows you to approach diverse challenges with confidence, equipped with a consistent and adaptable leadership tool kit.

Let's get started

Whether you're a new principal, an aspiring school leader, or a seasoned educator seeking fresh insights, this book is designed to be your companion, offering guidance and reflection as you navigate the challenges and joys of school leadership.

One of the most essential pieces of advice I can offer you is to approach this journey with a mindset of curiosity. School leadership is not about having all the answers; nor is it about following a prescribed set of rules. It is about staying open to learning, listening deeply to those around you, and continually asking questions that challenge your assumptions.

As you move through the chapters, you'll notice that many of the most influential leadership lessons come not from grand gestures or big decisions but from the quiet, everyday moments—greeting students at the door, offering a word of encouragement to a struggling teacher, or simply being present when someone needs to talk. These moments may seem small, but they are the building blocks of a compassionate school community. Leadership is about being present and available, knowing that your influence often lies in the simple act of showing up for others.

As you journey through these chapters, I encourage you to take time to reflect. Leadership is not a sprint but a marathon, and it's essential to carve out moments to pause, reflect, and recalibrate. Use the questions and prompts in each chapter for self-reflection. What insights resonate with you? Where are you challenged? What areas of your leadership practice need further attention or growth? Be honest with yourself, but also be kind. Leadership is a practice, and like any practice, it requires patience, self-compassion, and a commitment to continual learning. So, as you begin this journey through the 40 chapters, know that you are not alone. Use this book as a guide, mentor in print, and reminder that leadership, at its heart, is about helping others to do their very best. Lead with intention, lead with your heart, and trust that each step you take, no matter how small, is a step toward building a brighter, more inclusive future for your school community.

PART 1:

Authentic Leadership

Chapter 1

Architects of integrity: Building ethical leadership

Picture an architect meticulously creating the blueprint for a building. An architect ensures a building's foundation is stable, solid, and prepared to support the entire structure. For a principal, ethical leadership establishes the foundation of trust and transparency for the community. By openly communicating decisions, treating others fairly, and being transparent in their actions, principals assure staff, students, and parents that the school's "structure" is built on honesty and fairness.

Ethical blueprint design symbolizes ideals and principles rather than materials. This blueprint is more than just a plan; it's a responsibility and a commitment to lead the school with the highest ethical standards. In architecture, "integrity" refers to the structural strength of a building, guaranteeing safety and stability. For principals, integrity involves a firm dedication to ethical values and principles, ensuring that their decisions and actions align with their core values.

Integrity includes honesty, fairness, and consistency in words and actions. It implies using a moral compass to direct decision-making and upholding oneself to the highest ethical principles. This is crucial for a principal to maintain credibility and to make decisions that can withstand the scrutiny of the school community. When principals consistently uphold their values in policy enforcement and interactions with staff, they establish a trustworthy framework that staff and students can rely on. This framework should form the foundation of the principal's leadership and should be evident in their choices.

In architecture, the building code governs how buildings are designed, constructed, and maintained to ensure the public's safety, health, and welfare. In a school, a principal's ethical standards and core values provide the building code of a principal's leadership. But leadership cannot exist in isolation. An effective principal understands that their values must align with those of the staff, students, and broader school community to create a shared vision for the school's success. This alignment transforms ethical leadership into a collective effort, fostering buy-in, collaboration, and long-term sustainability.

One of the most impactful steps a principal can take is initiating open discussions with staff to identify shared values. These conversations allow the community to explore questions such as:

- What do we stand for as a school?
- What values guide our decisions?

By facilitating these conversations, principals help create a shared ethical framework that reflects the aspirations and beliefs of the entire school community. These then become the ethical standards—the building code—by which a principal can effectively lead the school community.

What this looks like

Aligning the blueprints: Honouring the collective core values

Architects must work with their clients to ensure a building's design reflects the needs and aspirations of its occupants. In a school, the principal must engage the school community to identify and honour shared core values. These collective values form the ethical foundation upon which the school's culture is built. A principal cannot simply impose their own values; rather, they must collaborate with staff, students, and families to define what matters most to the community, and seek alignment between their personal values and those of the collective. This alignment ensures that leadership decisions reflect not just the principal's integrity but also the values and aspirations of those they serve.

Designing with glass: Transparency in decision-making

An architect uses glass to invite in natural light and make the interior visible from the outside. Similarly, principals should lead with transparency, ensuring their decision-making is visible and understandable. Sharing the rationale behind decisions builds trust, even when those decisions are unpopular. Transparency doesn't guarantee agreement, but it does foster respect and acceptance when the community sees that decisions are grounded in fairness and thoughtfulness. This approach ensures that ethical leadership is as clear as a well-lit room, offering the school community insight into the principal's values and priorities.

Reinforcing the framework: Consistency in ethical practice

The strength of a building lies in the reinforced beams and columns that support its structure. Similarly, a principal demonstrates the strength of their integrity through consistent ethical behaviour in their daily interactions, whether addressing staff conflicts, student behaviour, or community relations. A principal's consistent responses to challenges help build trust and establish the principal as a dependable leader in times of stability and crisis.

Sustaining the structure: Commitment to ethical growth

Engineers regularly assess buildings to ensure their structural integrity and safety. Principals must do the same by periodically evaluating their leadership practices within their ethical standards. Ethical leadership requires an ongoing commitment to personal and professional growth, recognizing that the challenges of school leadership and societal norms and expectations are ever evolving. This commitment to ethical growth ensures the principal focuses on the present and is dedicated to reviewing and refining their long-term moral compass.

> Ethical leadership is the guiding principle that shapes the school's culture and future in every decision, interaction, and initiative. Principals who lead with integrity build a foundation that supports the present and secures the future, ensuring that their school remains a places of trust, respect, and ethical excellence.

Recognizing blind spots

Overlooking the substructure: The importance of core values

A building's strength is only as good as its foundation. For principals, this foundation is built on their core values. A common blind spot for principals is assuming these values are universally understood and embraced by the school community without regular reinforcement or assessment. Neglecting this foundational layer can gradually erode the principal's leadership effectiveness, much like unnoticed cracks in a building's foundation can compromise its entire structure. Principals must consistently reaffirm these values to maintain the structural integrity of their leadership.

Navigational challenges: Strategies for ethical dilemmas

Ethical dilemmas are not hypothetical exercises in school leadership—they are daily realities. Much like architects must decide how to balance safety, aesthetics, and cost when designing a building, principals must navigate decisions that weigh competing values: fairness and efficiency, discipline and compassion, policy and context.

There is no blueprint for these moments. Instead, principals must cultivate a set of strategies that allow them to move through ethical dilemmas with clarity and integrity. This begins with self-awareness—understanding how personal values, biases, and experiences shape decision-making. It also requires a deliberate approach to seeking multiple perspectives, ensuring that choices are informed by the collective wisdom of the school community rather than reactive impulses. Most importantly, ethical leadership is strengthened by consistency: when a principal has a clear moral compass and their decisions remain aligned with their deepest values, even when faced with difficult trade-offs.

Inconsistency in compliance to codes: Upholding ethical standards

One crucial challenge for leaders is being consistent in what they preach and what they practice. When principals advocate for honesty and fairness but fail to embody these values, it creates dissonance within the school community. Subtle biases and unconscious behaviour can seep into their decision-making, leading to favouritism or inequitable treatment. Principals must regularly examine their actions and decisions through an ethical lens, ensuring they uphold the same standards they expect from others.

Ethical leadership is more than making the "right" choices; it is about building and sustaining a resilient, compassionate, and unified school community.

Reflective prompts

Foundation check: Aligning ethics with professional actions

- What concrete steps have I taken to align my leadership actions with my ethical beliefs?
- How am I fostering ethical growth in my work?

Ensuring alignment between actions and beliefs allows principals to identify growth areas and reinforce their leadership foundation.

Load-bearing capacity: Balancing personal and professional demands

- Do my professional duties consistently reflect my values?
- How can I manage leadership pressures while staying true to my ethics?

By considering these questions, principals can reinforce their leadership's "load-bearing" strength and ensure that it remains resilient to the role's demands.

Elevating communication: Enhancing transparency and trust

- How transparent am I in decision-making?
- What steps have I taken to foster open, honest communication?

Clear communication strengthens trust and ensures that ethical practices are visible throughout the school community.

Strengthening accountability: Building a culture of responsibility

- How do I hold myself accountable for my decisions?

- What systems have I implemented to ensure accountability is a shared value within our school?

Accountability, modelled by the principal, fosters a shared culture of responsibility.

Through consistent reflection and adaptation, principals develop resilient leadership capable of meeting the complexities of their role. They create a school culture built on trust, ethics, and integrity—strong and enduring, like a well-constructed building.

Summary

Just as architects design buildings with careful attention to structure and aesthetics, principals must base their leadership on ethical integrity and core values. Principals who lead with integrity don't just follow ethical principles; they embody them, positively influencing the school community while ensuring stability and reassurance in the continually shifting landscape of school leadership.

When principals lead ethically, they demonstrate to the school community that actions rooted in honesty, empathy, and fairness are essential not only for personal success but for the collective well-being of all, which reassures the school community that integrity is modelled and celebrated. Ethical leadership is not just a choice—it's the foundation upon which lasting trust, stability, and school culture are built.

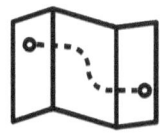

Chapter 2

Reading the landscape: Aligning maps and terrain

Imagine a principal navigating their school using a map. The map is familiar and comforting, even outlining what they believe to be the best routes for communication, decision-making, and problem-solving. It illustrates their strengths, intentions, and the leadership approach they think will successfully guide their staff and students. However, like any map, it is only a simplified representation of the actual terrain—a more complex, dynamic, and nuanced reality than the map can convey. The real-life landscape of a school encompasses diverse perspectives, emotions, and experiences that may not align with the principal's view.

In leadership, this gap between the map and the terrain is significant. A principal's internal perception of their leadership—the map—may not match how teachers, students, or parents experience it in the real world—the terrain. This metaphor of the map and terrain highlights a vital principle in leadership: self-awareness shapes the effectiveness of our actions.

For principals, the gap between how they perceive their leadership (the map) and how others experience it (the terrain) directly influences their ability to foster trust, motivate staff, and create a positive school culture. If a principal's map is outdated or inaccurate, it can lead to miscommunications, disengagement, and missed opportunities for growth within the school community.

Leadership experts Daniel Goleman, Richard Boyatzis, and Annie McKee reinforce this idea in their book *Primal Leadership*. They emphasize that self-awareness is the cornerstone of emotional intelligence and essential for effective leadership: "Without self-awareness, we are simply at the mercy of our internal states and drives, unable to manage ourselves or understand the impact we are having on others." This underscores that principals may believe they are effectively guiding the school when they lack the self-awareness to truly understand how their leadership is perceived by others.

In the broader context of leadership, self-awareness functions as a feedback loop that keeps principals grounded and aligned with their core purpose. It helps ensure their leadership is intentional, thoughtful, and consistently aligned with the school's mission and values.

Self-aware leaders understand that their map is incomplete and sometimes inaccurate, shaped by their own biases, assumptions, and blind spots. They recognize that their leadership may not always have the intended impact and that others might experience their leadership differently.

What this looks like

Plotting the course: Setting clear intentions

Self-aware leaders know what kind of environment they want to cultivate—whether it's collaboration, inclusivity, or academic excellence. These intentions serve as landmarks on their internal map, helping them navigate the many demands of school leadership. However, self-awareness requires revisiting and recalibrating these intentions to ensure they align with the school community's actual needs and realities.

Checking the map: Gathering feedback

Navigating school leadership without feedback is like using an old map to chart a new landscape—what once was accurate may no longer reflect the current terrain. For principals, gathering feedback is the act of updating the map. It reveals where they truly are, highlights changes in the environment, and helps them see whether their leadership direction aligns with the needs of staff, students, and families. Without regularly updating this map, leaders risk confidently moving forward while quietly drifting off course, unaware that the path they're following no longer leads where it once did.

Navigating rough terrain: Recognizing emotional triggers

Leadership challenges are like rough terrain, testing emotional resilience. A self-aware principal identifies emotional triggers, such as defensiveness or frustration, and avoids impulsive decisions. Instead, they pause, reflect, and respond thoughtfully, ensuring their leadership remains intentional and steady during challenging moments.

Updating the map: Adapting to new realities

No map is static, and the terrain of a school changes over time—new policies, shifting community dynamics, and evolving student needs require a principal to be adaptable. Self-awareness allows them to continually update their leadership map to reflect these changes. Self-aware principals don't cling to outdated practices but instead adjust their course as the terrain of the school shifts beneath them, ensuring their vision aligns with the school's real challenges and opportunities. Principals who lead with humility, adaptability, and clarity foster a school culture where everyone feels heard, valued, and empowered to succeed.

Recognizing blind spots

Unmarked obstacles: Overlooking the emotional climate

Sometimes, the emotional undercurrents in a school can be like unmarked obstacles on a map—hidden but still very real. A principal might focus so much on tasks, deadlines, or strategic initiatives that they overlook the emotional needs of their staff and students. Self-aware principals regularly check in with their school's emotional climate, recognizing that successful leadership requires not just achieving goals but also nurturing the well-being of the people around them.

Dead ends: Unquestioned assumptions

Unexamined assumptions can be dead ends in leadership. For example, assuming a particular communication style works universally may alienate those with different needs. Self-aware school leaders challenge their assumptions by seeking feedback and asking, "What perspectives am I overlooking?" or "Is this approach effective for everyone?"

Foggy vision: Misreading the experiences of others

Just as fog can obscure a traveller's view, principals may have a blind spot about how others experience their leadership. They may think they are providing clear direction or being supportive, but without asking for feedback, their understanding remains cloudy. For example, a principal may believe they are approachable, but if they are often rushed or distracted, others may experience them as distant or unresponsive. To avoid this foggy vision, principals must regularly seek out the perspectives of others to ensure their leadership is being received as intended.

Shortcut temptations: Micromanaging or overcontrol

When navigating complex terrain, shortcuts may seem appealing—but they often lead to trouble. Principals might think that stepping in and handling everything themselves is the quickest path to resolving issues. However, this approach can undermine trust, stifle staff autonomy, and create a culture of dependency. Self-aware principals recognize the value of empowering others to take ownership and make decisions, understanding that leadership isn't about control but cultivating growth and responsibility in others.

Unseen crossroads: Underestimating small interactions

Small interactions—whether a quick comment or hallway greeting—can significantly impact relationships and school culture. A rushed or dismissive response may unintentionally harm trust. Principals who value every interaction understand that even minor moments contribute to the school community's perception of leadership.

> Like skilled travellers, self-aware principals adjust their course by seeking feedback, reflecting on blind spots and remaining open to new perspectives. Self-awareness requires constant recalibration, ensuring a principal's internal map aligns with the school's lived realities.

Reflective prompts

Checking the coordinates: Clarifying your leadership intentions
- What are the core values driving my leadership decisions?
- Are these values evident to others in how I lead?

By asking these questions, principals can assess whether their leadership truly reflects their values, ensuring that their intentions match the direction they want to lead.

Surveying the terrain: Understanding staff and student needs
- What feedback has challenged my assumptions about staff or student needs?
- How might my leadership change if I focused more on unspoken or overlooked needs?

Reflecting on feedback encourages principals to consider the less visible concerns of quieter staff members or struggling students, fostering a more inclusive approach to addressing the school's needs.

Redrawing the map: Adapting to change
- When have I successfully adapted my leadership to address changing circumstances?
- Where might flexibility improve outcomes for the school community?

Leadership that resists change risks stagnation. Principals benefit from reflecting on where adaptability has fostered success and where rigidity may have hindered progress.

By regularly examining their leadership through these prompts, principals can align their internal intentions with the realities of their school community. This structured reflection helps ensure their actions, decisions, and impact remain purposeful and effective.

Summary

Leadership, like navigating unfamiliar terrain, requires more than a fixed map. The internal map that principals use to guide their decisions—their values, intentions, and leadership style—is essential, but it provides only part of the picture. To be effective, principals must consistently compare this map with the real-world terrain—the lived experiences, perceptions, and needs of their staff, students, and broader school community. Leading with self-awareness means recognizing that there will always be a gap between what a leader intends and how those intentions are received, and closing that gap is the key to successful, impactful leadership.

Principals who lead with self-awareness understand that their perception of events, decisions, and relationships is only one view of a multifaceted reality. These leaders expand their understanding of the actual terrain by routinely seeking feedback, listening to the quieter voices, and reflecting on their emotional responses. They become attuned to the subtle shifts and dynamics that shape the school environment, allowing them to respond with flexibility, empathy, and insight. This process requires looking outward—toward how others experience their leadership—and inward, with a willingness to challenge their assumptions and biases.

Chapter 3

Kintsugi leadership: Embracing the cracks

Imagine a broken decorative bowl carefully repaired with a special lacquer mixed with powdered gold and then placed on a shelf. While some might see the mended cracks as flaws that make the bowl less beautiful, others may view them as symbols of resilience, repair, and unique beauty. Kintsugi is the Japanese art of repairing broken pottery with gold, creating an entirely new piece of art. Kintsugi encourages embracing imperfections and vulnerabilities instead of hiding them, recognizing these aspects as part of a narrative of strength and renewal. According to kintsugi philosophy, the bowl doesn't lose its value or beauty; instead, it gains a new kind of grace and an individuality it didn't have when it was in its "perfect" state.

As a metaphor, kintsugi emphasizes the courage it takes to allow moments of vulnerability in a principal's leadership. The often prevailing belief implies that leaders should be invincible, projecting an image of unwavering confidence. This stereotype, somewhat embedded in school systems, puts pressure on principals and school leaders to maintain an image of flawlessness, placing a significant responsibility on them to lead stoically. Author Brené Brown has been a vocal advocate for the power of vulnerability. She says, "Vulnerability is not winning or losing; it's having the courage to show up and be seen when we have no control over the outcome." Her research emphasizes that vulnerability is an act of courage—a willingness to embrace uncertainty and exposure.

Why is this concept important for school leaders? Imagine what would happen if the leader of a school were to embody the spirit of kintsugi, to display their cracks—challenges, failures, and all—and lead not despite them but because of them. The example that sets for the school community is one of real, tangible humanity. It's an example that says, "I am not infallible, but I am always learning and growing." When leaders show their human side, they can connect more deeply with their staff and students.

By sharing these experiences openly, the principal encourages staff and students to adopt a growth mindset, where challenges are seen as stepping stones to improvement rather than obstacles. This vulnerability encourages teachers and students to view their own challenges as valuable experiences, fostering a school culture where everyone feels safe to take risks and learn from mistakes. Each misstep becomes part of a collective journey toward growth, much like each crack filled with gold in kintsugi contributes to the beauty of the final piece.

What this looks like

Acknowledging the cracks

A principal who embraces kintsugi-inspired leadership openly acknowledges their mistakes and uses them as teaching moments, showing the school community that errors are natural steps in the journey of growth. Rather than hiding or glossing over missteps, they share their experiences and the insights gained, setting a tone where vulnerability is respected and learning is continuous.

Displaying the cracks

Principals can openly express their vulnerability by sharing personal stories of setbacks and failures in various school settings. Leaders can effectively convey that setbacks are natural and essential to personal and professional growth by recounting specific instances where they faced professional challenges or stumbled significantly. Also, by articulating the valuable insights gained from these experiences, they can show that these setbacks have provided meaningful lessons.

Filling fractures with gold

Vulnerability in leadership means being open about one's imperfections and actively seeking and integrating feedback from the community to promote personal and professional growth. For instance, a school principal could seek input from their staff and students on their leadership style and use this feedback to guide their future actions and policies. These practices emphasize the importance of collective insight and highlight the leader's dedication to ongoing improvement and learning.

Reflecting light through the cracks

Incorporating reflective practices into the school culture can help destigmatize the act of embracing vulnerability. School principals could begin staff meetings with thought-provoking reflective questions, encouraging open dialogue about personal and professional growth. These opportunities allow individuals to connect with their own experiences, highlighting that acknowledging shared vulnerabilities can foster a sense of collective resilience and empowerment.

By leading with vulnerability, principals transform their schools into communities where imperfections become pathways to connection and progress. Like kintsugi, this approach turns cracks into sources of strength and beauty, reflecting the value of growth through authenticity.

Recognizing blind spots

Oversharing the cracks

While openness about challenges and mistakes is valuable, there is a fine line between being transparent and overwhelming others with too much information. Principals must be mindful of the context and the audience when sharing their vulnerabilities. They should aim to provide constructive and relevant insights, avoiding the trap of turning professional reflections into personal confessions that might erode their credibility or make others uncomfortable.

Allowing the gold to overshadow

It's important to not let a focus on personal vulnerability overshadow the contributions and vulnerabilities of others. Doing so can create a hierarchy of challenges where the leader's struggles are seen as more significant than others' in the school community. Effective vulnerable leadership involves balancing personal openness with attentiveness and responsiveness to the needs and vulnerabilities of the people they lead.

Misjudging the material

Different materials react differently to the kintsugi process, and different school cultures may respond differently to a leadership style that highlights vulnerability. Principals must demonstrate that, while they acknowledge their imperfections, they are still competent leaders. Pairing admissions of mistakes with explanations of the steps taken to address them and the lessons learned can maintain this balance. This approach reassures the school community that the leader is self-aware and proactive.

> For principals inspired by kintsugi, leading with vulnerability can significantly enhance school leadership, fostering a culture of empathy, resilience, and inclusivity. While embracing vulnerability can humanize and empower school leaders, navigating this approach with care and awareness is essential.

Reflective prompts

Evaluating the gold's application

- How can I share my struggles to build trust without undermining my credibility?
- How does my vulnerability impact team morale and trust levels?

Reflecting on these questions helps principals gauge the timing and context of sharing personal or professional challenges.

Judging the gold's weight
- How much of my struggles should I share to lead with vulnerability effectively?
- Does my openness encourage others to share, or does it unintentionally silence them?

Finding the balance between transparency and restraint ensures that vulnerability fosters a culture of mutual trust and learning.

Testing the strength of the repairs
- How has my vulnerability affected the school's culture?
- What specific feedback have I received about sharing my vulnerabilities?

Soliciting honest feedback from staff and stakeholders highlights areas where vulnerability strengthens connections or where adjustments are needed.

Assessing the material's readiness
- How ready is my school community to embrace vulnerability in my leadership?
- What steps can I take to prepare the school for this kind of leadership?

Assessing the current school culture and readiness for change involves understanding the existing levels of trust and openness.

> By pairing vulnerability with intentionality, principals can transform challenges into opportunities for connection and growth. Like kintsugi, this approach turns "cracks" into strengths, fostering a school culture where authenticity and professionalism thrive together.

Summary

The ancient Japanese art of kintsugi, which transforms cracks and imperfections, demonstrates that flaws are not just part of the journey—they can enhance beauty and value. Similarly, when principals embrace their vulnerability and make it visible to their school communities, they invite a culture of authenticity and growth. By leading with vulnerability, principals show that leadership does not require perfection; it thrives when individuals reveal their true selves, acknowledging their challenges and imperfections along the way.

By openly acknowledging mistakes and actively seeking input, principals create a culture where everyone—staff, students, and parents—feels valued and empowered to contribute. At its heart, kintsugi-inspired leadership reminds us that imperfections are not liabilities but opportunities to create something more substantial and meaningful.

Chapter 4

Bending without breaking: The resilient leader

Imagine standing in a bamboo grove, the stalks swaying during a heavy storm. Bamboo is known for its strength and flexibility, which protect it from storms and high winds. The bamboo plant serves as a metaphor for resilient leadership for school principals. Much like bamboo, a resilient principal is both grounded and adaptable, able to bend without breaking under pressure. This balance allows them to manage challenges with grace and perseverance, modelling the qualities of resilience for the entire school community.

Bamboo develops a strong underground root system before growing tall, and leaders should do the same: investing in both personal and professional growth to enhance their resilience. Research published in *The Leadership Quarterly* highlights that resilience is not innate but cultivated over time. Principals who prioritize self-development and relationship-building are better prepared to navigate the complexities of their leadership roles.

Bamboo thrives in diverse environments—from forests to rocky terrains—mirroring the adaptability required of principals in varied leadership contexts. Understanding the unique cultures, systems, and expectations of each school community allows principals to adjust their approaches effectively, transforming challenges into opportunities for growth.

Bamboo doesn't grow in isolation; it flourishes in groves, with each plant supporting and strengthening the others. Similarly, a resilient principal understands the importance of building a support network within the school community. By fostering strong relationships, open communication, and trust, they create a collective resilience that strengthens the school as a whole. This collaborative approach shows that resilience isn't just an individual trait but a shared quality that grows stronger together.

However, just as bamboo can bend only so far before breaking, principals must recognize their limits. Overextension risks compromising their well-being and effectiveness. Principals should assess the sustainability of their workload and adjust as needed—whether by delegating tasks, setting realistic deadlines, or temporarily stepping back from specific commitments. Flexibility in managing responsibilities is crucial for maintaining balance and long-term effectiveness.

Bamboo symbolizes the essence of resilient principal leadership: strength, flexibility, growth, and interconnectedness. By embracing these qualities, principals can navigate the complexities of their roles with confidence and purpose, cultivating a thriving school culture that adapts and evolves to meet its challenges.

What this looks like

Thriving in diversity: Adapting to different environments
Bamboo thrives in diverse conditions, showcasing remarkable adaptability, a trait principals should attempt to adopt when transitioning to new leadership settings. By actively listening, conducting needs assessments, and being culturally aware, principals can effectively refine their approach to leading their schools. Entering a new leadership setting is like a young bamboo shoot establishing itself in unfamiliar soil. It takes time to develop a deep, interconnected root system, and new principals should set realistic expectations, allowing themselves time to understand their new environment and build strong relationships. It's important to remember that growth and stability come gradually, requiring patience and consistent effort.

Cultivating flexibility: Adapting to educational winds
Resilient principals understand that change is inevitable and approach it flexibly. They are open to new ideas and are willing to adjust their strategies. This flexibility allows them to adapt to new teaching methods, curriculum updates, and technological advancements without losing sight of their

school's goals. By remaining open and adaptable, they can turn potential disruptions into opportunities for growth and improvement.

Growing together: Fostering interconnectedness

Bamboo grows in clusters, with each stalk connected through a network of roots, illustrating the importance of community and collaboration. For principals, fostering a sense of interconnectedness within the school enables shared goals and collective achievements. This involves creating spaces for open dialogue, encouraging feedback, and providing professional development opportunities that equip staff to handle change. By nurturing a culture of mutual support and continuous learning, principals can empower their teams to adapt and thrive in new environments.

> When leaders show they can handle change with grace and determination, they encourage others to adopt a similar approach. This leadership style turns resilience into a shared value, where the school community thrives together, like a grove of bamboo that bends but doesn't break, regardless of the circumstances.

Recognizing blind spots

Overrelying on strength and flexibility

A significant blind spot is the tendency to overlook the emotional toll that change can take on staff and students. While focusing on strategic planning and implementation, principals may underestimate the anxiety, resistance, and fatigue accompanying transitions. Leaders must acknowledge these emotional responses and provide adequate support, such as counselling services, professional development on stress management, and opportunities for open dialogue.

Misinterpreting resilience as inflexibility

For school principals, it is essential to differentiate between resilience and resistance to change. When bamboo bends without breaking, it doesn't always return to its original form; rather, it adapts to a new shape as circumstances may demand. It's crucial to understand that true resilience involves adaptability—knowing when to stand firm and when to embrace new directions for the growth and benefit of the school community.

Neglecting the underlying root system

Principals who adapt quickly to change may expect the same level of flexibility from their teachers and staff without considering individual differences in coping mechanisms and learning curves. School leaders should recognize that each team member may require different support and more time to adjust. Differentiated professional development, peer mentoring, and a culture of patience and understanding can help bridge this gap.

Underestimating the need for renewal

Bamboo's incredible ability for rapid renewal and growth shows its resilience. A principal's blind spot may be underestimating the importance of self-renewal and continuous learning. In school leadership, relying on past achievements or becoming complacent with current knowledge and skills can impede progress. Principals should adopt a mindset of lifelong learning and pursue new experiences and insights that can revitalize their leadership and motivate their school communities.

> Recognizing and mitigating these potential pitfalls ensures their leadership is adaptive and empathetic, fostering a school environment prepared to thrive in the face of change.

Reflective prompts

Swaying with flexibility: Adapting to change
- How have I adjusted my leadership style to meet this year's challenges?
- In what ways have I upheld our school's core values while implementing change?

Like the bamboo that thrives by bending in the wind, principals must demonstrate flexibility without compromising their foundational principles.

Rooted in strength: Anchoring leadership
- What are the foundational values that anchor my leadership?
- How do these values shape my interactions with staff and students?

Like the roots of bamboo, a leader's strength is grounded in deeply held values that provide stability and guidance.

Enduring the storm: Managing adversity
- How do I respond to adversity, and what does this reveal about my leadership?
- What significant challenges have I faced this year, and how did I address them?

A leader who understands how they deal with adversity will help better inform their response during challenging times.

Growing toward the sun: Pursuing improvement
- In what areas have I seen the most personal and professional growth this year?
- What goals have I set for further development, and how will I achieve them?

The growth of bamboo is both upward and expansive, suggesting continual improvement.

> The resilience, flexibility, and interconnectedness of a bamboo grove offer a model for school leadership. Through regular reflection and a commitment to growth, principals can navigate challenges, inspire their communities, and lead with strength and grace.

Summary

Resilience is a vital attribute for principals, anchoring their leadership in strength, adaptability, and purpose. Much like bamboo that bends without breaking and thrives in diverse conditions, resilient principals create a school culture that withstands challenges, embraces change, and supports the growth of every individual within the community.

Interconnectedness plays a crucial role in a principal's resilience. Like the extensive root system of bamboo, resilient principals benefit from fostering impactful professional networks. These networks provide them with essential support, valuable advice, and resource access, enhancing their capacity to lead effectively and make informed decisions.

Resilient leaders understand that change is a constant and inevitable part of their role. Like bamboo that bends gracefully without breaking, school leaders should embrace change and adjust their strategies and approaches to meet new challenges and opportunities. This adaptability ensures their survival and serves as a model of resilience for their entire school community. Resilient leaders can turn challenges into growth opportunities by remaining open to new ideas, innovative practices, and diverse perspectives, nurturing a culture of continuous improvement and learning.

Chapter 5

Rest as rhythm: Strategic pauses

In a piece of music, the rests are just as important as the notes themselves. A well-placed rest creates space, tension, and anticipation, allowing the melody to breathe and the listener to reflect on what has just been played. Without pauses, music would be chaotic and overwhelming, lacking the rhythm and flow that make it impactful.

In the same way, the strategic use of pauses and rest is essential in a principal's day. These breaks are not interruptions but intentional moments that allow the principal to reset, recharge, and refocus—making their leadership more sustainable and effective and supporting their well-being. Like the rests in a powerful musical composition, pauses throughout a principal's day bring clarity, depth, and balance to their work.

This holistic approach to work and leadership challenges the traditional notion of constant productivity. A piece of music without rests lacks rhythm; it feels rushed and chaotic. Likewise, a principal's day without pauses can feel overwhelming and unbalanced. Strategic pauses and moments of rest are essential to effective school leadership. They enhance decision-making, improve emotional intelligence, foster presence, and create a sense of rhythm that prevents burnout.

A principal who moves at full speed all day may appear engaged, but without moments to pause, they risk being physically present yet mentally absent. Teachers sense when a leader is distracted or merely going through the motions. When leaders are fully present, they create spaces where others feel heard, valued, and supported—fostering a stronger, more connected school culture.

Principals can build pauses into their day without disrupting their workflow. Simple shifts—like taking a few deep breaths before a meeting, walking slowly between classrooms rather than rushing, or closing the office door for five minutes of quiet reflection—can create space for clarity and balance. Scheduling time for deep work, where emails and interruptions are paused, allows for more focused decision-making. Even small acts, like choosing to listen fully before responding, can transform a principal's leadership presence.

However, in the demanding world of school leadership, the reality is that principals often find themselves with little time to pause. The urgency of daily crises, unexpected challenges, and the need to be constantly available can make it feel impossible to step away or take even a brief moment to catch their breath. This lack of space is not a reflection of poor planning or priorities but a natural consequence of the role's intensity. While intentional pauses are ideal, principals must also find ways to embrace micro-moments of rest—brief but meaningful pauses between tasks or meetings—that allow them to recalibrate without disrupting the flow of their day. Though fleeting, these small acts of self-care can be just as impactful as longer breaks, creating a rhythm amid the chaos and enabling principals to sustain their leadership amid the demands of the role.

What this looks like

Starting the day with quiet preparation

In a musical piece, the opening notes set the tone for everything that follows. In a principal's day, the first moments are crucial for establishing a positive and intentional rhythm. Principals who incorporate strategic pauses often start their day with a few minutes of quiet preparation—arriving at school early to enjoy a cup of coffee in silence, reviewing their schedule, and mentally preparing for the day's challenges.

Midday resets for energy and focus

In a well-composed piece of music, a rest provides a sense of balance and gives the melody room to breathe. Principals can incorporate this concept by creating midday resets—intentional pauses that allow them to step away from the intensity of the day and restore their energy. These breaks can be as simple as a short walk around the school grounds or a few minutes of mindfulness practice in a calm space. This midday reset enables the principal to approach the second half of the day with renewed focus and patience. They ensure the principal maintains the energy needed to handle the demands of the afternoon and model a healthy balance for staff and students.

Practising intentional reflection

Just as a rest in music allows both the performer and the listener to reflect on the melody, strategic pauses give principals time to reflect on their leadership. This reflection doesn't have to be lengthy or formal—it can be a few quiet moments at the end of the day to think about what went well, what was challenging, and what could be improved. This reflective pause can help them process the day's events and consider how they want to approach similar situations in the future. It's a way of "reviewing the score" before moving on to the next day's melody, ensuring that leadership constantly evolves and improves.

Closing with intention

A principal benefits from an intentional ending to their day. Before transitioning to personal time, taking a brief pause to acknowledge successes, recognize staff contributions, and express gratitude can create a sense of fulfillment. This transition period helps principals mentally leave work at school, ensuring they can fully engage in their personal lives. By closing the day with intention, they foster a healthy work-life balance and set an example for the school community.

> Strategic pauses and moments of rest are essential elements to a principal's leadership; they bring clarity, depth, and purpose to the role. Much like the rests in a beautiful piece of music, these intentional breaks create space for reflection, connection, and presence, allowing the principal to lead with focus and resilience.

Recognizing blind spots

Perception versus reality: When rest is seen as a disconnect
A principal who frequently takes time away from the busy school environment—whether to reflect, recharge, or reset—might be perceived by staff, students, or parents as being distant or disconnected from the school's daily life. This misunderstanding can lead to a sense of inaccessibility, creating the impression that the principal is not actively involved in the immediate challenges of the school community.

Overscheduling pauses
While structured pauses are beneficial, an overly strict approach can lead to a loss of spontaneity and flexibility, which are crucial in a dynamic school environment. A principal who is too focused on maintaining scheduled pauses may miss unexpected opportunities for meaningful interactions or timely decision-making. Recognizing that some days may require more spontaneous responses, principals can build in the habit of pausing while remaining open to the unexpected demands of school life.

Using pauses as avoidance
Strategic pauses can unintentionally become a form of avoidance if they are used to delay or escape from challenging situations. While pauses are helpful for managing emotions and gaining perspective, they should not be used to delay necessary actions. Principals need to strike a balance between taking time to reflect and knowing when it's essential to face challenges head-on, ensuring that pauses serve as preparation for engagement rather than a means of avoidance.

Losing momentum
In music, rests are carefully placed to enhance the flow of the piece, but if they are too frequent or poorly placed, they can interrupt the rhythm. Similarly, if a principal's pauses are too frequent or disruptively timed, they can hinder productivity and the day's natural flow. Understanding the right timing for pauses ensures that they serve their purpose without diminishing productivity.

Strategic pauses and moments of rest are powerful tools for effective leadership, but they require a mindful and intentional approach to avoid common pitfalls. This mindful balance is what makes rest not just a break from leadership but an integral part of it, supporting a sustainable and impactful school culture.

Reflective prompts

Creating space for reflection: Is my "rest" enhancing the flow?
- Am I using pauses strategically to create space for reflection, or are they disrupting the flow of my day?
- Do I intentionally choose moments to pause that help me gain clarity, and make better decisions?

Principals can ensure they are creating space for thoughtful reflection without losing momentum by evaluating the timing and purpose of their pauses.

Maintaining balance: Are my pauses serving the whole composition?
- Am I balancing my moments of rest with the needs of the school community, ensuring that my pauses benefit not only me but also those I lead?
- Do I model the importance of rest in a way that creates a culture that values self-care and balance?

Just as rests in music contribute to the overall beauty of the piece, a principal's pauses should serve the well-being of the entire school.

Engaging in intentional rest: Am I choosing the right moments to pause?
- Do I pause after particularly stressful situations, allowing myself to reset before moving forward?
- Do I create space in my schedule to intentionally reflect on my leadership, using pauses to assess what is working well and what could be improved?

Purposeful pauses—much like rests in music—highlight critical moments, offering a chance to process and respond thoughtfully. Strategic reflection during these pauses enhances a principal's capacity to lead with clarity and poise.

Adjusting for rhythm: Am I flexible with my pauses?
- Can I adjust the timing and length of my pauses to meet the unexpected demands of the day, or do I adhere too rigidly to a set schedule?
- Do I remain adaptable in my approach to rest, recognizing when it's time to take an unplanned pause or to shift a scheduled one based on the needs of the moment?

These questions focus on flexibility in incorporating pauses into the daily leadership rhythm. In a musical composition, the timing of rests can be adjusted for dramatic effect, depending on the flow of the piece.

> Strategic pauses are the rests that bring rhythm, balance, and depth to a principal's leadership. Through thoughtful reflection, principals can make the most of their moments of rest, leading with a rhythm that is both sustainable and impactful and creating a school culture that values well-being, presence, and continuous growth.

Summary

Strategic pauses are more than breaks in the busy schedule of a principal; they are vital components of effective and sustainable leadership. A musical rest creates space for reflection, anticipation, and deeper appreciation of the following notes; a principal's moments of pause bring clarity, presence, and balance to their day. These intentional breaks are not a sign of weakness or disengagement but rather an act of leadership wisdom—ensuring that each decision, conversation, and action is grounded, thoughtful, and aligned with the school's vision.

By pausing strategically, principals enhance their ability to make better decisions, manage stress, and remain emotionally attuned to their community's needs. Pauses allow for moments of reflection, where principals can assess what is working, identify what needs to change, and refine their leadership practices based on the lessons learned. Strategic pauses acknowledge that leadership, like a well-composed piece of music, requires action and reflection, intensity and stillness, sound and silence.

Chapter 6

Guiding the way: The lighthouse of curiosity

In school leadership, curiosity acts like a lighthouse—illuminating uncharted waters, guiding the way forward, and helping to navigate both calm and stormy seas. A principal who leads with curiosity shines a light on the unknown, asking questions, seeking understanding, and exploring new possibilities. Curiosity provides clarity in moments of uncertainty, ensuring that the school stays on course even when the path ahead isn't clear.

The quote "Be curious, not judgmental," often attributed to Walt Whitman, captures the essence of curiosity-driven leadership, highlighting the importance of approaching situations with openness. A principal who embodies this mindset creates a school environment where inquiry, exploration, and diverse perspectives are valued—leading to more thoughtful decisions and a more inclusive community.

A principal who leads with curiosity approaches challenges, conflicts, and opportunities with a desire to understand before responding. This means asking questions, gathering information, and listening deeply to the perspectives of staff, students, and parents. For example, when faced with a drop in student performance, a curious principal doesn't rush to conclusions or blame. Instead, they explore the issue, asking questions like, "What factors might be contributing to this decline?" or "How do different students experience our teaching methods?" This light of curiosity reveals the situation's complexities, allowing the principal to gain insight before taking action. It helps the school community navigate challenges with clarity and informed decision-making.

Being curious is essential for dealing with the complexities of educational reform and policy changes. According to the Association for Supervision and Curriculum Development (ASCD), leaders who approach reforms with a curious mindset are better equipped to adapt to changes and implement new strategies effectively. They are more likely to seek new information and perspectives to inform their decision-making process.

A lighthouse exposes hidden dangers, revealing rocks and obstacles that could otherwise go unnoticed. Curiosity in leadership functions similarly—challenging assumptions, uncovering biases, and illuminating blind spots that might hinder the school's progress. A principal who leads with curiosity doesn't settle for surface-level explanations but digs deeper, asking probing questions to uncover the root causes of issues and seeking diverse perspectives to broaden their understanding.

What this looks like

Anchoring in values: Aligning actions with beliefs

Curiosity-driven leaders anchor their actions in core values like a lighthouse grounded on a solid foundation. Principals leading from a place of curiosity understand the importance of aligning their leadership practices with their core beliefs and values. This alignment ensures that the light of curiosity shines consistently and authentically, guiding the school community with integrity and purpose.

Illuminating challenges: Solving problems with compassion

Curiosity, like a lighthouse, illuminates hidden obstacles. Leaders who embrace curiosity don't just see problems as hurdles to overcome but as opportunities to better understand and support their school community. By attentively listening to the perspectives of staff and students, they better understand the root causes of challenges. This approach may enable them to develop solutions that are better aligned with the school's culture and be more successful in finding solutions to the less apparent obstacles hindering the school's progress.

CHAPTER 6

Casting light over dark waters: Seeking to understand before acting
Leading with curiosity means examining the unknown before making decisions. A curious principal prioritizes understanding and clarity, taking time to gather information, listen to various perspectives, and explore the complexities of a situation before acting. This approach leads to more informed, thoughtful decisions that align with the school's mission and values.

Illuminating new paths: Encouraging exploration and innovation
A lighthouse not only warns of dangers but also reveals new pathways and possibilities. Similarly, a curious principal encourages the school community to explore uncharted territory, take risks, and innovate. They value experimentation, foster creativity, and provide the freedom to try new approaches without fear of failure. They facilitate spaces where staff can collaborate, share what they're learning, and reflect on their experiences. Questions like, "What have you noticed about the impact of this new strategy?" or "How could we tweak this approach to better fit our students' needs?" drive the inquiry process. This openness to experimentation lights the way for continual improvement and innovation, helping the school community find better ways to serve its students.

> A principal who leads with curiosity illuminates challenges and opportunities, helping the school navigate the unknown with clarity and confidence. This type of leadership is characterized by a commitment to understanding, a willingness to explore, and an openness to new ideas.

Recognizing blind spots

Shining too brightly: Overwhelming staff with questions
A lighthouse beam needs to be carefully calibrated: too bright, and it can disorient or overwhelm. Similarly, a principal who leads with excessive curiosity may bombard staff, students, or parents with too many questions, requests for feedback, or inquiries. While the intention is to gather insight

and promote understanding, this can cause fatigue or frustration, leaving the school community feeling overanalyzed and under pressure.

Focusing too narrowly: Missing the bigger picture

A lighthouse beam lights a specific area, leaving others in shadow. When principals are overly focused on particular issues, curiosity can create a similar effect. Principals who dive deeply into isolated concerns may lose sight of broader trends, interconnected problems, or the school's overarching goals. This narrow focus can lead to an imbalance in leadership priorities, with critical areas being overlooked. Effective leaders must balance detailed exploration with a wide-angle perspective to ensure holistic understanding and alignment with the school's mission.

Getting lost in a fog of familiarity: Overlooking diversity

A beacon's light may dim when the fog of familiarity is present. Surrounding oneself with like-minded individuals can create an echo chamber where only similar ideas are supported. This can lead to one-sided decisions that do not fully address the school community's needs. To break through this fog, principals must actively encourage various viewpoints in discussions and foster a culture that welcomes and actively seeks a spectrum of views. Curiosity plays a vital role in this process, as it encourages leaders to actively seek out and consider diverse perspectives, enriching the decision-making process.

Blinding others with the light: Discouraging dialogue

A lighthouse beam is intense, and if shined directly into someone's eyes, it can be blinding. Similarly, if not handled carefully, a principal's curiosity can come across as intense or intimidating, discouraging others from speaking openly. This can happen when curiosity takes the form of relentless questioning, or if the principal's enthusiasm for exploration inadvertently overshadows the voices of staff or students. This can create a culture where dialogue is stifled, and individuals feel that their input is not valued. To avoid this blind spot, principals should focus on creating a safe and welcoming environment for inquiry, ensuring that curiosity fosters genuine dialogue rather than shutting it down.

CHAPTER 6

Curiosity-driven leadership is powerful and transformative, much like the guiding light of a lighthouse. Curiosity should guide the principal's actions, inform their decisions, and inspire the collective vision of the school community.

Reflective prompts

Beacon of purpose: Is my curiosity focused?
- Am I directing my curiosity toward specific goals that align with our school's mission, or am I exploring topics without a clear purpose?
- When I ask questions, do I have a well-defined reason behind them, and am I clear about what I hope to learn from the answers?

A lighthouse beam needs to be carefully aimed to be effective; likewise, a principal's curiosity should be focused on areas that matter most for the school's success.

Igniting the beacon: Cultivating a culture of inquiry
- How can I create an environment where teachers and students can ask challenging questions?
- How can I better model a spirit of inquiry in my daily interactions with staff and students?

Leaders need to foster an atmosphere of openness and security to create a culture of inquiry that welcomes challenging questions and encourages risk-taking.

Illuminating the dark corners: Addressing hidden issues?
- Am I using my curiosity to explore areas that might be overlooked or uncomfortable to address, or am I focusing only on what's easy or familiar?
- Do I seek out diverse perspectives that might challenge my assumptions and provide new insights, or do I rely on the same sources of information?

A lighthouse reveals dangers that are not easily seen, and a principal's curiosity should serve the same purpose—casting light on areas that might otherwise go unnoticed.

Lighting new trails: Adapting to change

- How can I better prepare for and adapt to the changing educational landscape and its challenges?
- What strategies can I implement to integrate new instructional practices while maintaining the quality and integrity of our current programs?

When nurtured, curiosity becomes a beacon that guides leaders and their communities through the ever-evolving educational landscape.

> Leading with curiosity is about more than asking questions—it is about guiding the school community with a clear, purposeful light that illuminates the path ahead. The journey of leading with curiosity is one of continual exploration and adaptation, and reflective questions are the checkpoints that help principals stay on course.

Summary

Leading with curiosity is not just a leadership strategy; it is a mindset—a way of being that values inquiry, understanding, and openness above all else. Much like a lighthouse that stands tall in turbulent seas, a principal who leads with curiosity illuminates the path for their school, guiding the community through both calm and stormy times.

Leading with curiosity is about recognizing that leadership is not a static endeavour but a living, breathing process of exploration, questioning, and learning. A curious principal understands that every challenge is an opportunity to learn, every setback a chance to grow, and every success a step toward greater knowledge.

As principals continue to lead with curiosity, they model the courage to ask difficult questions, the patience to seek understanding, and the resilience to navigate uncertainty.

Chapter 7

The blueprint of leadership: Developing your brand

Imagine strolling through the streets of Paris and catching sight of the Eiffel Tower standing proudly against the skyline. Or picture the Empire State Building in New York City, a timeless symbol of architectural expertise and cultural importance. These well-known structures are more than just buildings; they embody their respective city's spirit, history, and ambitions.

A principal's leadership brand is much like an iconic building in a city's skyline—it stands out, it is recognizable, and it helps define the school's and community's identity. Just as landmarks give character to a city, a principal's leadership brand gives shape and meaning to the school's culture. It becomes a symbol of the values, vision, and leadership style of the principal, setting them apart and making their leadership instantly recognizable to students, staff, and the broader community.

A principal's brand reflects what they do, how they do it, and the lasting impression they create. People perceive a principal's leadership brand based on their values and the impact they have on their school community. Often, principals within the same jurisdiction are likely to be compared to one another inside and outside the school communities they lead.

Whether focusing on innovation, equity, or community building, a well-defined leadership brand helps a principal create a lasting impression, ensuring their leadership is memorable and impactful. The principal's clear and visible leadership identity shape a school's culture and direction.

When a principal clearly defines their values and vision—whether it's creating a culture of collaboration or championing student-centred learning—staff, students, and parents are more likely to align themselves with these goals. The principal's leadership brand acts as a guidepost, helping others understand the school's direction and what it stands for. This consistency in leadership strengthens trust and builds cohesion within the community.

It is important to note that the opposite can also occur. Like a rundown building, the principal whose leadership is, at best, questionable can establish a negative brand. This can be a significant challenge for school leaders. Maintaining an iconic landmark like the Empire State Building is much easier than transforming a dilapidated, poorly maintained structure into an iconic building. It is the same with the leadership brands of school principals; sustaining a positive brand is much easier than renovating a negative one.

Developing a personal brand as a school principal is about aligning values with actions and leaving a positive imprint on the school community. A principal's personal leadership brand is the legacy built and the story told through their leadership.

What this looks like

Blueprint for integrity

"Structural integrity" refers to the leader's consistent embodiment of their values and beliefs in their actions and decisions. It highlights the importance of their consistency in their leadership branding, which is essential for building trust and credibility within the school community. Like a building's foundation, a principal's leadership brand should be sturdy, clearly defined, and represented in every decision and interaction.

Architectural vision

An architect envisions a building that complements its environment, and a principal should design their leadership brand to align with and enhance the school's mission. This involves being strategic about how their values integrate with their school's goals, shaping a forward-thinking learning environment. The principal's vision for the school becomes a scaffold supporting the community's aspirations, similar to an iconic building that positively impacts a city's pride and spirit.

Withstanding the elements
Whether facing a crisis, navigating change, or responding to conflict, a principal who has built a strong leadership brand can rely on their core values to guide them. For instance, a principal whose brand centres on resilience and empathy will lead with calm assurance during a crisis, offering support and guidance to staff and students while maintaining a clear focus on solutions. The principal's brand is a beacon of stability, much like a well-constructed landmark building that stands firm through turbulent weather.

Becoming a lasting landmark
Over time, the principal's brand becomes embedded in the culture of the school, influencing how staff lead, how students learn, and how the community views the school. Even after the principal moves on, their leadership legacy remains, much like a landmark building that continues to shape the city long after its construction. By investing in and nurturing their leadership brand, a principal ensures that their influence endures for future leaders to build on.

> These core values consistently demonstrate how the principal communicates, makes decisions, and interacts with staff, students, and the community. A principal who clearly defines their values provides a steady base that shapes their leadership and helps others understand the essence of their brand.

Recognizing blind spots

Avoiding architectural rigidity
A building with a fixed design may struggle to accommodate new uses, and a principal's brand that is too rigid can become outdated. A lack of adaptability may hinder the brand's evolution in response to the changing needs of

the school community. Principals should focus on maintaining an adaptable brand that reflects the evolving needs of students and staff.

Overshadowing the landscape

The design of a unique building might overshadow or clash with its surroundings, and a principal's strong brand might overshadow or suppress the development of distributed leadership within the school. Principals should nurture an environment where they spread leadership opportunities throughout the school, ensuring that their brand enhances rather than overshadows the leadership of others.

Creating an illusion of transparency

The principal's brand is like a building with a reflective glass facade: it looks attractive but might not show what's inside. This can create a false sense of transparency, making it hard for people to see what's happening. Similarly, a principal's brand might seem open and engaging, but it could lack transparency, leading to distrust and disconnection in the school community. Principals should ensure genuine communication and actions so their brand builds trust and authenticity.

Standing out on the skyline: Overlooking how others perceive you

A principal's leadership brand may not be seen the way they expect. For example, a principal who believes their brand is centred on approachability might not realize their demeanour in high-stress situations makes them seem distant or unapproachable. The blind spot is in assuming self-perception equals public perception.

> Creating a personal leadership brand as a school principal requires thoughtful consideration of how this brand influences the school environment. Like an iconic building, a leadership brand must be consistently aligned with its foundation, adaptable to changing conditions, and nurtured from within.

Reflective prompts

Blueprint integrity
- How does my leadership brand align with the school's vision?
- How can I reinforce the structural elements of my leadership brand to support the school's culture?

An architect ensures the blueprint reflects the intended purpose and aesthetics of a building; a principal must consider how their leadership brand and strategies align with their vision for the school's culture.

Load-bearing walls
- Which elements of my leadership carry the most weight in achieving the school's goals?
- Where might there be a gap between how I want to be perceived and how I actually lead?

Great design has a unified look and feel—so should a principal's leadership.

Acoustic design
- Have I effectively communicated the values that underpin my leadership brand?
- Do my decisions and actions consistently reflect the values I want my leadership to represent?

These questions encourage principals to reflect on whether the foundation of their leadership brand—its core values—has been clearly communicated and consistently demonstrated.

Standing out on the skyline
- How do others perceive my leadership brand, and does it align with my intended image?
- What feedback from staff, students, and the community informs my leadership identity?

Like an iconic building that stands out in the skyline, a principal's leadership brand should be recognizable and positively associated with the school's culture.

> When a principal establishes a brand that embodies values like integrity, inclusivity, and collaboration, they send a clear message about their leadership intentions. This alignment fosters a sense of trust and cohesion among students, staff, and families, much as an iconic structure can inspire pride and unity within a city.

Summary

A principal's leadership brand is the cornerstone of their identity and influence within the school community. Like an iconic building that defines the skyline, a well-developed leadership brand distinguishes a principal, making their values, vision, and actions recognizable and impactful.

However, a leadership brand isn't just about visibility or recognition, it's also about authenticity. A principal's brand must be built on a foundation of core values and reinforced by daily actions that reflect those principles. Declaring a vision is not enough; principals must live it in every decision and interaction.

At the same time, a leadership brand must evolve. Just as a landmark building requires maintenance and updates to stay relevant in a changing world, a principal must adapt their leadership to meet the evolving needs of the school, staff, and students. Flexibility, resilience, and a commitment to growth are essential elements of a leadership brand that can endure the test of time.

Ultimately, the most impactful leadership brands are those that outlast the leader. By consciously building, maintaining, and evolving their leadership brand, principals elevate their leadership and create a foundation for lasting success within their schools.

Chapter 8

Gratitude: The rechargeable energy of leadership

Batteries are necessary energy sources for everyday devices, such as remote controls and smoke detectors. Their primary function is to store and deliver consistent, reliable power, ensuring that devices operate effectively. A principal's gratitude can be likened to a battery, as it serves as a source of positive energy for the school community. A battery supplies energy to keep devices running smoothly, and gratitude supplies the emotional and psychological energy that keeps teachers, staff, students, and parents engaged, motivated, and connected. In the often-demanding environment of a school, where stress and fatigue can quickly drain enthusiasm and spirit, gratitude acts as a revitalizing force, renewing energy and reinforcing the school's collective sense of purpose.

Gratitude is one of the most powerful renewable energy sources a principal can tap into. It fuels leadership, sustaining a school leader through inevitable challenges and uncertainties. And when other sources are low, gratitude replenishes a principal's emotional reserves, helping them stay grounded, resilient, and connected to their purpose.

Batteries also enable devices to communicate with each other, from remote controls working with televisions to Bluetooth devices pairing with smartphones. Gratitude also facilitates better communication and stronger relationships within the school. A principal's thankful demeanour strengthens the connection between staff and students, like a battery maintaining the connection between different device parts.

Research in positive psychology and organizational behaviour consistently shows the significant impact of gratitude on leadership effectiveness. A study conducted in 2003 by psychologists Robert Emmons and Michael McCullough revealed that individuals who regularly practised gratitude experienced improved psychological well-being, better physical health, and enhanced interpersonal relationships. For school principals, these advantages result in improved stress management, increased job satisfaction, and a more united school community.

Gratitude also has a multiplier effect; it doesn't just replenish the principal's energy, it spreads through the entire school and beyond, energizing staff, students, and families. A simple acknowledgment of a teacher's hard work or a genuine thank-you to a student for their effort can recharge others' batteries, too.

What this looks like

Recharging relationships: The rejuvenating power of appreciation

Gratitude helps principals stay connected to their purpose. When the daily grind of leadership becomes challenging, gratitude is a reminder of why they chose this path in the first place. Every moment of appreciation—whether for a staff member who went above and beyond or for a small act of kindness from a student—grounds the principal in the joy and fulfillment of their role. This connection to purpose is like an energy reserve that keeps leadership sustainable.

Optimizing performance: The boost of gratitude

A battery boosts the performance of the device it powers; a principal's visible expression of gratitude can increase the performance of the entire school community. When staff and students genuinely feel appreciated, they can be empowered to give their best, nurtured with a sense of ownership and satisfaction in their work.

CHAPTER 8

Storing potential: The reserve power of gratitude
A principal's visible appreciation creates a reserve of goodwill and positive morale that can be tapped into during difficult times, similar to how a battery stores energy for later use. This reserve is essential for helping the school handle external pressures and navigate internal challenges. It is a source of resilience, enabling a positive response when unexpected obstacles arise.

> Leading with gratitude can help create a positive school atmosphere, turn potential into reality, and build reserves for tough times.

Recognizing blind spots

Overcharging: The risk of inauthenticity
Leaving a battery charging for too long can cause damage or reduce efficiency, just as constantly or excessively expressing gratitude can risk coming across as inauthentic or insincere. When gratitude feels continuous but lacks depth or sincerity, it can lead to cynicism and decreased trust in leadership. Genuine gratitude is specific and arises from a true appreciation for the work and effort of others rather than being generic praise. It's crucial to ensure that expressions of gratitude are always sincere and meaningful.

Corrosion: The erosion of impact over time
Proper battery maintenance is essential to prevent corrosion, which can decrease performance. Similarly, the efficacy of expressing gratitude may diminish if it becomes predictable or if the school community becomes desensitized to it. To prevent erosion, principals should diversify how and when they communicate gratitude to ensure it remains impactful and fresh.

Leakage: The diffusion of focus
When a battery leaks, it loses its ability to charge a device effectively. When gratitude is vague or unfocused, it loses its power to positively impact individuals. Expressing gratitude in a general or all-encompassing way without

acknowledging specific individuals or actions can result in a lack of personal connection and reduced effectiveness. Principals should express gratitude in a targeted and specific manner by linking their appreciation to particular actions or behaviour.

Discharge rate: Balancing immediate and delayed expressions of gratitude

The discharge rate of a battery shows how quickly it releases its stored energy. This is like expressing gratitude, as it's crucial to balance immediate, spontaneous thanks with delayed, more reflective appreciation. Immediate gratitude can quickly boost a team's morale, while delayed gratitude offers more profound, thoughtful recognition. Balancing these approaches ensures that gratitude can act as both an immediate motivator and a lasting source of positive reinforcement.

> When practised thoughtfully, gratitude becomes a powerful tool to energize and sustain the school community. Principals who lead with authentic and balanced gratitude create a culture of positivity, trust, and lasting engagement.

Reflective prompts

Voltage drops: Maintaining consistent gratitude
- Have fluctuations in my mood or external pressures affected the frequency of my gratitude?
- How can I ensure my gratitude remains consistent and reliable?

Maintaining consistent gratitude helps build trust and ensures that gratitude's positive effects are reliable, enhancing the overall school climate.

Monitoring the discharge rate: Balancing spontaneous and reflective gratitude
- Do I balance spontaneous expressions of gratitude with more thoughtful acknowledgments?

- How can I ensure my gratitude is both timely and impactful?

Balancing instances of spontaneous and reflective gratitude enhances sincerity and serves as both an immediate motivator and a thoughtful reinforcement.

Avoiding overheating: Preventing gratitude burnout

- Have I observed signs of cynicism about gratitude practices among staff?
- How can I ensure my expressions of gratitude remain genuine and well received?

Ensuring genuine, not excessive, gratitude, can help maintain its positive impact without leading to fatigue or cynicism among staff and students.

Checking for leakage: Ensuring focused and specific gratitude

- Is my gratitude specific enough so that it resonates personally with its recipients?
- How can I improve my gratitude's specificity to ensure it truly resonates with each individual?

Specificity ensures gratitude feels personal and genuine, helping individuals feel valued and appreciated.

This reflective practice guarantees that leading with gratitude continues to have a meaningful impact.

Summary

A device's optimal functioning relies on a stable and continuous energy flow provided by a battery. Similarly, a principal's consistent expressions of gratitude are a source of positive energy that keeps the school running smoothly. Leading with appreciation can energize a school community.

Rechargeable batteries have the feature of being renewable, providing a sustainable power source. Principals can adopt this attribute by regularly replenishing their gratitude reserves. Gratitude isn't a finite resource but a renewable one. Reflection, positive interactions, and acknowledging the successes and efforts of others regenerate it. By recharging their approach with gratitude, principals ensure that their leadership continues to motivate others, preventing burnout and nurturing a resilient school culture.

Similar to how a battery optimizes the performance of the devices it powers, making them more efficient and effective, gratitude optimizes the school's performance. It improves efficiency by boosting morale and motivation.

PART 2:

Visionary Leadership

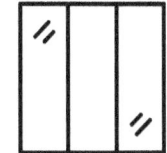

Chapter 9

The mirror and the window: Developing a vision

Picture a principal positioned between two walls: a mirror is on one wall and a window on the other. In this example, these are not just objects but metaphors that capture the essence of developing a vision. With its reflective surface, the mirror depicts the school as it is—its strengths, challenges, heart, and soul. It offers an unfiltered view of the present, with every flattering or harsh detail visible. This mirror requires honesty and introspection, compelling the leader to face the realities of their school community. The window on the wall opposite is not just any window, but one that provides a glimpse into an unwritten future. It's the school as it could be. It represents potential and possibility. It's an invitation to imagine and strive for the desired future beyond the horizon.

The mirror reflects the school's current state—its culture, achievements, and challenges—providing a clear and accurate picture of the school community. This reflection grounds the community, ensuring all members know the starting point. The window offers a view into the possible futures, projecting what the school community might become.

The mirror shows the principal where the school excels and where it falls short. It encourages them to ask questions such as, "Are we meeting our students' needs?" "Does our school culture support learning and growth?" and "What are the underlying challenges within our walls?" This reflection helps address weaknesses and ensures ongoing development and improvement.

The window pushes the principal to dream of a better future and guide the school community toward that vision. It raises the questions, "What can our school become?" and "How can we better serve our students and our community?"

It is important for a principal to balance these two insights. Solely depending on reflection can result in a leadership approach that is trapped in daily responsibilities and without a future outlook. On the other hand, focusing only on visioning might result in setting unrealistic goals that don't align with the school's actual capabilities and needs. This can lead to initiatives that aren't practical or sustainable.

To navigate this dynamic effectively, a principal must weave reflection and vision into a cohesive leadership strategy. Reflection grounds leadership in the present, while vision inspires and mobilizes the school community by providing a shared sense of purpose and direction. It pushes boundaries and encourages innovation, helping the school to evolve and thrive.

Creating a vision for a school is an essential part of effective principal leadership. The metaphor of a window and a mirror illustrates the dual focus that brings this vision to life. Together, the window and mirror create a balanced approach to vision-setting, allowing the principal to lead with both inspiration and realism.

What this looks like

Reflective leadership through the mirror

Using the mirror metaphor for leadership, a principal demonstrates openness and genuineness by acknowledging the school's strengths and weaknesses. This transparency fosters trust and strong relationships among staff, students, and parents. By openly addressing challenges and celebrating successes, the principal ensures a shared understanding of the school's current and future needs.

Visionary leadership through the window

Using the window metaphor helps the principal communicate a vision for the future and transform aspirations into practical, strategic objectives. This forward-thinking leadership involves presenting a realistic path ahead rather than an unattainable dream. By clearly articulating objectives and framing the future through this window, the principal can better guide the school community toward common goals with greater clarity.

Setting realistic goals that bridge the mirror and the window

Principals who balance reflection and vision set realistic, collaborative goals that link the present to the future. These goals address immediate needs while advancing long-term aspirations. For instance, fostering a collaborative school culture might start with increasing team-based professional development or creating shared planning times. Aligning goals with current capabilities and future potential keeps the school community motivated and focused on progress.

Balancing the mirror and the window

Balancing the mirror's clarity with the window's foresight ensures that a school's vision remains both ambitious and achievable. A principal must constantly toggle between assessing present conditions and inspiring future possibilities. When executed effectively, this balance creates a shared sense of purpose, empowering the school community to work together toward a future that is both visionary and grounded in reality.

> A principal who leads with the clarity of a mirror demonstrates honesty, transparency, and awareness. Combining this with the foresight of a window enables them to anticipate challenges and inspire the school community to achieve a shared vision.

Recognizing blind spots

Overlooking the silent challenges

The mirror reflects visible aspects of school life—academic performance, teacher engagement, and student success—but it can miss hidden issues. Staff burnout, subtle student disengagement, or underlying inequities often remain beneath the surface. If left unrecognized, these silent challenges can weaken the school's foundation. Principals must foster open communication channels, regularly gather qualitative feedback, and actively observe the nuances of daily interactions within the school community to uncover issues that might not be immediately apparent in data or metrics.

Chasing unattainable horizons: Beyond the window

The window inspires school principals to imagine an ambitious future. Still, it can also create blind spots by presenting goals that may be unattainable given the school's current realities. A vision that doesn't consider the school's resources, the community's needs, or potential external constraints can lead to more aspirational than operational strategies, creating a gap between what the school envisions and what it can achieve.

Resistance to both perspectives

Principals may overlook their staff's resistance to accept the school's current reality or embrace change to move the school forward. It is not unusual for members of the school community to have very different views about the current challenges for the school and the direction in which it should grow. Despite a vision that promises a bright future, entrenched school community habits and a prevailing culture of resistance can impede forward momentum. It is crucial to pinpoint and confront the underlying reasons for this resistance, whether it is fear of the unfamiliar, a lack of trust, or insufficient support for the vision.

> Principals should balance the realities in the mirror with the possibilities in the window. By transparently sharing assessments of the present and articulating an achievable vision, they can foster a school culture that is grounded in its current situation yet inspired by future potential.

Reflective prompts

Reflecting through the mirror: Understanding our current reality
- What reflections in the mirror of our school am I avoiding or not seeing clearly?
- How accurately does the mirror reflect the experiences of everyone in our school community?

Honest reflection helps identify real challenges and opportunities, ensuring strategies and actions are rooted in the school's true needs, not partial or biased perceptions.

Gazing through the window: Envisioning what we can become
- What future possibilities do I see through the window, and how do they align with our school's core values and mission?
- How do I discover what is not currently in my view?

Aligning the vision with the school's mission fosters purpose and direction, inspiring collective effort toward shared goals.

Balancing the mirror and the window: Harmonizing vision and reality
- How can insights from the mirror refine our vision, ensuring goals are aspirational yet realistic?
- How can I engage others in embracing and contributing to the vision?

This balance is essential for fostering a visionary leadership style deeply connected to the school's immediate needs and long-term goals.

> By regularly reflecting on these questions, principals can lead with clarity and purpose. Drawing on insights from the mirror and aspirations from the window, they can guide their schools toward a thriving future.

Summary

The mirror and window metaphor provides a framework for principals to balance reflection and vision in their leadership. The mirror allows principals to confront their school's current state honestly and transparently, recognizing strengths and areas for improvement.

Through the window, principals envision a hopeful future, inspiring the school community to work toward shared goals. Turning aspirations into actionable plans, this forward-thinking perspective drives progress.

Relying solely on one perspective can undermine leadership. Without the window, the mirror may lead to overly critical or stagnant leadership, focused only on the present. Without the mirror, the window may result in lofty goals disconnected from reality, leading to unachievable or unsustainable initiatives. Balancing the two ensures that insights from the mirror inform the vision through the window.

Leading with both perspectives transforms a principal's vision from abstract goals into realistic actions and genuine community engagement. It fosters resilience, optimism, and dedication, guiding the school toward growth one thoughtful step at a time. A principal who balances the mirror and window creates a meaningful journey toward progress and a school environment where everyone sees their reflection in both the present and the future.

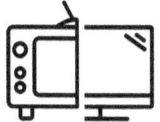

Chapter 10

Bridging eras: Integrating tradition with modernity

In cities where old and new buildings coexist, there may be a historic cathedral standing next to a sleek, modern art museum. Both structures represent essential aspects of a vibrant cityscape: the cathedral is revered for its timeless history, while the museum attracts visitors with its contemporary creativity. The contrast between the two serves as a metaphor for the delicate task that school principals often face when they blend time-honoured traditions with more progressive approaches.

For principals, balancing tradition with modernity in their schools is akin to bridging the old and the new, ensuring both have a place and purpose in the school community. In recent years, leadership literature has focused on adaptive leadership, emphasizing the importance of being flexible and responsive to change. In the book *The Practice of Adaptive Leadership*, the authors argue that effective leadership involves solving problems and navigating the complexities of change while balancing tradition and innovation.

To effectively navigate the blending of the old with the new, principals must have a deep understanding and appreciation for the value of traditions within their schools. These traditions are the threads that connect the school's past to its present and often provide stability and predictability for the school community. However, this respect for tradition should not prevent adopting new practices and perspectives.

While traditions often do provide stability, it is essential to remember that progressive change will become the traditions of the future. Gradual change is often more effective than a radical overhaul. A gradual approach with an acceptable timeline for implementation, which is usually dictated by the school community, allows everyone to adapt to change without feeling overwhelmed or disconnected from the school's core values. Taking small steps toward a larger goal can ensure everyone is on board and comfortable with the change, and the transition becomes smoother and more manageable.

This approach allows for the creation of a school culture that honours its past while stepping into the future. Like the cathedral and the museum standing in harmony, a school that successfully balances tradition with innovation allows the roots of history to support the wings of progress.

What this looks like

Integrating traditions with modernity through curation

Principals play a vital role in shaping school culture by curating a balance between past and present. This might involve updating longstanding policies to meet current needs or blending traditional practices with innovative strategies to foster student success. Like an architect who preserves a cathedral's historical significance while incorporating modern design, the principal ensures that tradition and progress coexist harmoniously.

Communicating the evolution

Effective communication is a crucial part of this leadership style. Like guiding visitors through a museum, the principal should regularly provide updates through newsletters, social media, or meetings. These updates explain how any initiatives relate to the school's values and build on past successes. This ongoing conversation ensures transparency and keeps everyone informed and engaged in the continual development of the school community.

Celebrating cornerstones and keystones

Recognizing and celebrating traditional and innovative achievements within the school community is similar to an architect highlighting critical elements of a structure that contribute to its uniqueness and functionality. Awards ceremonies, feature articles in school publications, and special recognitions in assemblies celebrate both time-honoured practices and fresh approaches, making the principal's balanced leadership approach visible to the entire school community.

> Honouring the past while embracing innovation creates a dynamic learning environment that respects tradition while fostering growth. This approach ensures the school remains rooted in its heritage while thriving in the future.

Recognizing blind spots

Overvaluing tradition
While respecting school traditions is vital, an overattachment to the past can hinder progress. Principals may resist necessary changes, such as adopting research-based practices, out of a desire to maintain "the way things have always been." This reverence for tradition can inadvertently sustain outdated methods that no longer serve the school's best interests, limiting its ability to adapt to new educational demands.

Overlooking core traditions
Modernizing a school doesn't mean abandoning tradition; it means finding ways to integrate innovation with respect for the past. Neglecting traditions can undermine the school's historical integrity. An architect who places too much emphasis on innovative elements might compromise a building's historical authenticity, and a principal who focuses excessively on innovation risks might erode the goodwill of the community that comes with respecting the traditions of the school that have developed over time.

Introducing imbalance
School leaders should balance traditional and modern teaching methods like an architect skillfully integrates contemporary elements into a historic building. They must thoughtfully influence teaching methodologies with fresher approaches to maintain a cohesive learning experience. This will

likely require the principal to set realistic timelines for implementation and provide professional learning support to ensure a successful transition.

Getting caught in preservation paralysis

When school principals are too focused on preserving the school's historical identity, they may experience preservation paralysis, making it difficult to make necessary and much-needed changes. This can hinder the school's ability to adapt and meet the students' current needs. Small, incremental changes that occur in a structured timeline can help ease the possible paralysis that may set in when implementing modern approaches.

> Principals, like architects, must skillfully balance tradition with innovation to build schools that honour legacy while embracing the future. By blending historical strengths with forward-thinking approaches, they create progressive, responsive learning environments that meet the needs of their students and communities.

Reflective prompts

Assessing the blueprint of innovation

- Which innovations align with our school's history and current needs?
- How do I decide which new approaches to integrate?

These reflections ensure new practices complement the school's culture and address educational demands without conflicting with longstanding traditions.

Structural integrity check

- Are initiatives enhancing learning while maintaining core traditions?
- How can I assess their impact on our school's values?

Evaluating the effects of innovations ensures they uphold the school's identity while enriching the learning experience.

Harmonizing the old and new
- How can we thoughtfully integrate traditional and modern elements?
- What steps ensure this balance is seamless?

Harmonizing old with new creates a cohesive environment where tradition and innovation support one another.

Future-proofing the design
- What are the long-term implications of these changes?
- How can I sustain both innovations and valued traditions?

Focusing on sustainability ensures changes align with both immediate needs and long-term goals.

Navigating change with compassion
- How do I address resistance to new initiatives?
- What strategies support transition for those aligned with traditional practices?

Managing resistance with empathy ensures smoother transitions while maintaining respect for all perspectives.

> The most effective school leaders are those who can look to the past with gratitude and to the future with vision. They understand that tradition and innovation are not opposing forces but complementary elements that, when balanced, can enrich the school community.

Summary

Just as a cityscape can blend an ancient cathedral with a modern art museum, a school must mix its historical identity with innovative practices. This requires a principal to act with understanding and foresight, ensuring the school's foundational traditions are honoured and maintained.

At the heart of this leadership lies a deep respect for tradition. School traditions are the threads that weave together generations, creating a sense of continuity, belonging, and pride. They tell the story of the school's values and culture, and for many members of the community, they hold deep emotional significance.

However, tradition alone cannot sustain a school in an evolving world. Modern educational practices, emerging technologies, and new pedagogical approaches are essential for preparing students for future success. Embracing innovation is not about abandoning tradition but enhancing the educational experience in relevant and forward-thinking ways. Respecting traditions while modernizing the school is about understanding that these two elements are not in opposition but part of a cohesive whole. Both can exist proudly together, each telling their own story while contributing to a broader narrative of growth, learning, and community.

Chapter 11

Orchestral harmony: Balancing management and vision

Imagine a school as an orchestra, with the principal as the conductor. Each instrument represents a part of the school—teachers, students, staff, parents, and extracurricular activities. The principal must ensure each section is in tune and playing cohesively, creating a harmonious symphony. This metaphor illustrates the balance principals must strike between managing daily operations and providing visionary leadership to foster a positive school culture.

Management tasks—such as budgeting, scheduling, and policy enforcement—are like tuning instruments: essential for smooth operations. As has been noted by James Spillane and colleagues, effective management is critical for a school's functioning. Like an out-of-tune orchestra, a poorly managed school will struggle regardless of how skilled the teachers are.

However, leadership goes beyond management. It includes setting a vision, inspiring staff, and fostering a culture that maximizes learning. Like a conductor interpreting a music score, the principal leads the school community to create something more significant than the sum of its parts. Michael Fullan, in his book *Leading in a Culture of Change*, highlights the principal's role as an agent of change, guiding the school toward a shared vision.

Efficient management can free a principal's time and energy for visionary tasks. Well-run systems reduce operational issues, allowing more focus on long-term goals. Balancing these roles is key, and reflection is crucial to maintain this balance. A conductor reviews performances, noting successes and areas for improvement. Similarly, principals benefit from assessing their school's operations and culture, identifying what's working and where adjustments are needed. This reflective practice enables continuous growth and fine-tuning of leadership.

Extending this metaphor of the harmonious orchestra, the audience is the school community—students, staff, parents, and stakeholders invested in its success. It's the conductor's job to read the audience's reactions, and the principal's job to respond to the school community's needs and expectations.

Balancing management and leadership requires skill, attention, and purpose. By coordinating operational tasks with inspirational leadership, principals create a "performance" that runs smoothly and inspires all involved. Ensuring each section is in tune, setting a steady tempo, empowering key players, and harmonizing vision with action are the hallmarks of effective school leadership.

What this looks like

Setting the tone: Establishing a clear rhythm

Like a conductor setting the tempo, a principal who leads in this way establishes clear expectations and routines that keep the school community in sync. This means communicating a daily rhythm through organized schedules, well-structured meetings, and consistent practices that allow each part of the school to function smoothly. By setting a steady pace, the principal ensures that teachers, students, and staff have a predictable and supportive environment in which to operate.

Leading with purpose: The principal's vision

To the school community, the principal's leadership is like the conductor's vision for a performance. It guides the direction and ensures everyone achieves a common goal. The vision creates a shared sense of purpose that everyone can rally behind. When the principal has a clear vision, it gives the school community something to strive for. Teachers feel connected to a bigger picture, students understand what they're working toward, and parents feel confident that the school is on the right path.

CHAPTER 11

Managing with precision: The importance of fine-tuning
While vision provides direction, effective management ensures everything runs smoothly. Scheduling, budgeting, and upholding policies are the practical skills of the principal that keep the school functioning. Like a conductor's precise use of the baton, strong management allows teachers to teach, students to learn, and parents to trust in the school's operations. These day-to-day details build a stable environment where everyone can thrive.

Finding the balance: Leading and managing together
Every day, a principal needs to bring leadership *and* management to the job, especially when the need for a decisive moment in the "performance" of the school is called for. These are the moments when the principal's ability to balance vision and practicality shines—guiding the school through a challenging situation or pushing forward with an initiative. The whole school community can feel this balance when the principal strikes it well; in those moments, the school is confident that it's moving in harmony.

Knowing when to change the tempo: Adapting to the moment
An experienced principal, like a professional conductor, knows when to lead from the front and when to focus on the more minor details. Flexibility is critical to maintaining the balance between leadership and management. This requires a principal to be agile in their approach to leadership and be willing and able to pivot quickly when the school community needs them to do so. Adaptability helps create a sense of stability and confidence in the school's direction.

> Balancing leadership and management is challenging, but when done well, it transforms a school. A principal who excels at both roles fosters trust, inspires confidence, and creates an adaptable, forward-moving environment for their school community.

Recognizing blind spots

Overplaying the melody: When vision drowns out the details

The melody is vital, but without harmony and rhythm, the music loses depth. Similarly, principals who are overly focused on vision may need to pay more attention to immediate needs. This might look like a principal full of ideas but struggling with follow-through, leading to frustration and mistrust. Ignoring operational details like scheduling or teacher support can alienate the school community. To maintain trust, principals must balance big-picture goals with the school's day-to-day pulse.

Micromanaging the sections: Stifling creative expression

A conductor must trust the musicians to play their parts; a principal must resist the urge to micromanage every detail of the school's operations. A principal who is overly controlling can stifle creativity and innovation among staff. The larger school community might see micromanaging as a lack of trust, leading to low morale and disengagement. Principals must recognize when they're overstepping and trust their team to handle specific tasks. Effective delegation and empowering staff to take ownership of their roles help create a more dynamic and positive school culture.

Losing the rhythm: School discord

A conductor must stay connected to the orchestra's rhythm, feeling the pulse of the music and responding in real time. A rhythmic blind spot can appear when a principal is so focused on leadership strategies or management metrics that they lose sight of what's happening in classrooms and hallways. When this happens, the school community might view the principal as being out of touch, and may create a sense of alienation and frustration. Staying attuned to the rhythm of the school—by engaging regularly with teachers, students, and staff—ensures the principal's leadership remains relevant and responsive to the school's needs.

CHAPTER 11

Chasing crescendos: The temptation of quick fixes
Crescendos in music bring excitement, but if there are too many, their impact is diminished. Similarly, principals may chase quick fixes—immediate, impressive changes that fail to address deeper issues. Some problems require urgent response, but relying too heavily on quick fixes can lead to cycles of temporary solutions without lasting progress. Strategic planning ensures that each "crescendo" supports the school's long-term goals.

By staying mindful of these pitfalls—overemphasizing vision, micromanaging, disconnecting from the school's rhythm, and chasing quick fixes—principals can lead with balance. A principal's steady hand ensures that every note contributes to a harmonious and thriving school community.

Reflective prompts

Tuning the instruments: Aligning vision and practice
- Do my daily decisions support our long-term vision?
- How often do I revisit our vision to ensure it's reflected in our daily operations?

Like instruments that must be tuned before a performance, a principal's day-to-day decisions must be in tune with the school's long-term goals.

Balancing the sections: Leading versus managing
- Am I giving enough time to both lead and manage, or am I favouring one?
- How do I divide my energy between big-picture goals and operational details?

In an orchestra, neglecting one section weakens the whole. Similarly, focusing too much on leadership or management can disrupt a school's balance.

How am I interpreting the score?
- Am I too rigidly following policies, or do I adapt to my school community's unique needs?
- How flexible is my leadership style in addressing challenges and opportunities?

Adapting leadership styles to changing circumstances ensures responsiveness to new challenges and maximizes opportunities for growth and improvement.

Do I listen to the orchestra as much as I lead it?
- How open am I to feedback from my staff, students, and the wider community?
- Am I approachable and receptive to new ideas and criticisms?

A good conductor listens closely, and principals must do the same. Gathering feedback ensures that leadership resonates with the entire school community.

Is the orchestra's performance continually improving?
- What measures do I use to assess the impact of my leadership and management on school outcomes?
- What have been the tangible results of balancing these roles?

Understanding outcomes provides valuable insights to guide future strategies and improve performance.

> Balancing leadership and management is like fine-tuning an instrument—ensuring everything is in sync and performing at its best. Regular reflection helps principals maintain harmony, align their efforts with shared goals, and foster a school community that moves forward with clarity and purpose.

Summary

Like a conductor, a principal must unite diverse elements—teachers, students, staff, and the broader community. Balancing visionary leadership with precise management is challenging but essential for creating a thriving school environment. When principals lead with care and attention, each part of the school works in tune, contributing to a performance greater than the sum of its parts.

Effective school leadership goes beyond following the score. It involves listening to the ensemble, adapting to the moment, and ensuring every community member feels valued and understood. Meticulous management prevents operational issues from overshadowing the school's mission, freeing principals to focus on building a positive culture, driving innovation, and inspiring their teams.

A principal who balances leadership and management fosters trust, collaboration, and continual improvement, guiding the school toward its goals. This is the art of school leadership—inspiring, managing, leading, and listening to create a symphony of excellence that resonates throughout the school community.

Chapter 12

Ripples of influence: Small actions, big impacts

Imagine a calm lake reflecting the sky. When a small pebble drops into the still water, it creates ripples that spread outward, reaching every corner of the lake. In school leadership, small changes work the same way. Even minor adjustments—whether in routines, relationships, or culture—can generate a ripple effect that profoundly impacts the school community over time. By understanding and leveraging this effect, principals can guide meaningful change without overwhelming staff, fostering growth with sustainable momentum.

Small changes are a powerful tool for leadership. Each decision, no matter how minor, has the potential to spark significant transformations. Shifting the focus from large-scale reforms to steady, incremental progress allows leaders to appreciate how minor adjustments can drive long-term improvement.

One challenge of making small changes is that their impact isn't always immediately visible. Leaders must learn to recognize the long-term potential of these adjustments to see the broader shifts they create. For example, encouraging teachers to share resources more effectively may seem small, but it can foster a culture of collaboration that strengthens the learning community over time.

School leaders often face pressure for quick results, but real and lasting change takes time, and patience is essential when implementing small changes. This requires trusting the process and staying focused on long-term goals, even when immediate outcomes aren't evident. Effective leadership involves nurturing these small changes to align with the school's broader vision.

Another critical aspect of leading through small changes is maintaining momentum. Leaders must establish systems to monitor progress, gather feedback, and make necessary adjustments. Consistency in promoting these changes ensures they take root, while clear communication reinforces how each small action supports the school's overall goals.

By considering the ripple effect in their school, a principal can reflect on any small actions already in motion. Perhaps it's the way they greet staff each morning, the moment they pause to acknowledge a teacher's effort, or the choice to ask a thoughtful question instead of offering an answer. These seemingly minor acts generate trust and connection, cultivating a culture where growth is possible.

Leadership is not about monumental shifts but about the intentionality behind each interaction. Principals can deepen their presence and alignment with their school's vision through small, steady actions. By recognizing the power of these ripples, they create the conditions for others to thrive and the entire community to flourish. Just as a pebble impacts an entire lake, thoughtful, incremental actions can inspire trust, build momentum, and transform a school from within.

What this looks like

Dropping the pebble: Initiating visible change

The first step involves implementing an intentional, visible change, such as introducing a new collaborative tool or organizing regular feedback sessions. This action should be clearly communicated to staff, students, and parents, explaining its purpose and anticipated outcomes. This transparency builds excitement and engagement from the outset.

The first waves: Immediate impacts

Initial results appear closest to the core, showing immediate, observable impacts. Early successes encourage and validate change, and sharing these achievements—through newsletters or assemblies—reinforces the value of the initiative and demonstrates progress to the school community.

CHAPTER 12

Widening circles: Extending the influence
As the ripples extend, their influence reaches broader areas of the school. A successful initiative can inspire similar approaches among staff, fostering a culture of shared learning and collaboration. Principals can amplify this impact by encouraging adoption, providing resources, and supporting adaptation to scale the benefits across the school.

Reflecting the sky: Aligning with broader goals
As the ripples spread, staff and students begin to embrace the transformation, and the principal continues to guide efforts to ensure it aligns with the school's overarching vision. Each new wave of change strengthens this connection and drives further progress.

> The ripple effect in school leadership demonstrates how small, intentional actions can profoundly transform a school's culture, influence practices, and align the community with broader goals. These seemingly minor changes create momentum, shaping the school environment in meaningful and enduring ways.

Recognizing blind spots

Submerged rocks: Overlooking immediate needs
Focusing on gradual, long-term change risks overlooking urgent issues requiring immediate attention. These hidden challenges can disrupt progress and undermine broader efforts. Principals must remain vigilant, continuously monitoring the school environment to address pressing needs while steering incremental improvements.

The undertow: Resistance to change
Resistance, like an undertow, can quietly undermine change efforts. Staff who are reluctant to abandon established routines or community members who feel excluded may hinder progress. Engaging stakeholders early,

fostering clear communication, and emphasizing the benefits of change can mitigate this resistance and build collective support.

Diverging currents: Misalignment of goals

As changes ripple outward, they may shift in unintended directions. For example, initiatives like increasing collaborative teaching time might inadvertently lead to higher workloads and lower morale. Principals must monitor outcomes closely and adjust to keep initiatives aligned with the school's goals and values.

Shadows and reflections: Miscommunication and misperception

Misunderstandings can distort the intentions behind changes much like shadows and reflections can misrepresent reality. Clear, consistent communication and regular check-ins help clarify intentions, address concerns, and prevent confusion from escalating.

> By addressing these hidden challenges, principals can enhance the effectiveness of ripple-effect leadership. Combining small, consistent actions with decisive interventions ensures meaningful change, alignment with long-term goals, and a resilient, engaged school community.

Reflective prompts

Dropping the first pebble: Setting intentional actions

- What recent actions have I taken to create a positive learning atmosphere for staff and students?
- How intentional are these actions, and do they align with the school's broader goals?

When chosen strategically, small actions have a meaningful impact. Reflecting on their purpose ensures that each "pebble" aligns with the school's vision and creates lasting positive ripples.

CHAPTER 12

Submerged rocks: Addressing the most pressing needs
- What urgent issues (submerged rocks) exist in our school?
- How effectively are my initiatives addressing these priorities?

Focusing on critical needs ensures that leadership actions resonate throughout the school and address immediate challenges.

The undertow: Understanding resistance
- What undertow of resistance have I encountered with recent changes?
- How can I effectively engage stakeholders to reduce resistance and increase buy-in?

By understanding and addressing the sources of resistance, principals can better engage resisters more effectively.

Reflections and shadows: Managing unintended consequences
- What unexpected outcomes have arisen from recent changes, and how have they affected our school?
- How can I address any adverse consequences of these initiatives?

Unintended consequences offer valuable learning opportunities. Reflecting on them helps principals mitigate negative effects and refine strategies for future success.

> By engaging with these reflective questions, principals ensure their actions create intentional, positive ripples that progressively shape the school's culture and achievements.

Summary

The ripple effect metaphor illustrates how small, deliberate actions by school principals can lead to significant changes within a school community. Every decision, no matter how minor, has the potential to create widespread and lasting impacts. As small pebbles create expanding concentric circles that may touch every part of a lake, minor school changes can lead to sweeping transformations.

Each small action a principal takes—whether recognizing a teacher's effort, fostering collaboration, or celebrating wins—sets off a ripple that builds a supportive, resilient school environment. This approach emphasizes the necessity of daily interactions and intentional decisions to cultivate trust, motivation, and a shared sense of commitment to the school's vision. Through these consistent, thoughtful actions, principals demonstrate that leadership is not only about the grand gestures but also about the everyday moments that shape the character and success of the school. By embracing the power of incremental change, principals can foster sustainable, transformative change, demonstrating that every journey starts with a single step or a pebble.

Chapter 13

Horizon leadership: Balancing the good and the bad

Imagine a navigator standing on the deck of a ship, gazing out toward the horizon. At a distance, the horizon may seem deceptively close or, at times, impossibly far. However, seasoned navigators realize that the horizon's appearance can be misleading, and they must maintain perspective to guide their vessel wisely through changing seas.

Like a navigator, a principal should understand that the initial impression of a situation—whether overwhelmingly positive or disastrously negative—often doesn't reflect the whole picture. Circumstances in a school are nuanced and layered, and responding impulsively based on first impressions can lead to decisions that may be out of sync with the true scope of the issue.

Thinking about this metaphorical horizon helps principals maintain a balanced perspective. They understand that the daily challenges and successes are just part of a more extensive journey and that each day brings opportunities and challenges, many of which are not as significant as they may initially appear.

A broad perspective is not just a leadership mindset; it's a tool for making better decisions. When faced with a difficult staff conflict, an angry parent, or a sudden policy shift, a principal who understands the full landscape doesn't react impulsively. Instead, they pause, gather information, and consider both immediate and long-term consequences. They ask themselves, "Will this issue still feel urgent a month from now?" "How does my response today impact trust, relationships, and the school's future direction?" Perspective allows principals to lead with intention rather than react to the loudest or most pressing problem at hand.

When viewed from a distance, these issues become part of a much larger landscape, including the school's overall health, students' progress, and the school community's long-term goals. By stepping back and gaining a more expansive view, a principal can see that what feels critical at the moment is often just one piece of a much bigger picture, allowing them to navigate in a more measured way.

For a principal, this means leading with patience and empathy, understanding that today's urgent matters will eventually become part of the school's ongoing narrative. This approach encourages both proactive and forward-thinking leadership while still valuing patience and contemplation.

A principal who understands that seldom is anything as good or as bad as it appears is like a seasoned navigator guiding their ship. They value the moments of calm but are always preparing for what lies ahead. They endure storms with resilience, knowing that rough seas are often temporary.

What this looks like

Perspective leadership: Steering clear of extremes

A balanced perspective fosters stability for staff and students. It allows principals to have an evenhanded outlook, preventing them from becoming overly complacent during successes or disheartened by setbacks. It encourages flexible, thoughtful leadership focusing on the school's long-term journey.

Navigating transitions: Guiding through change

The context of school leadership changes with new policies, student needs, and community expectations. By focusing on the long-term, principals can lead transitions that are less reactive to immediate fluctuations and more responsive to the school's enduring needs and goals. This ensures that the school effectively adapts to change with consistent leadership.

Looking to the horizon: Seeing beyond the immediate

The horizon symbolizes both what we can see and the vast possibilities beyond. In moments of success, such as high test scores or community accomplishments, it reminds us that these achievements are milestones, not endpoints. Similarly, during challenges like budget constraints or staffing issues, it offers reassurance that obstacles are temporary and part of a more significant journey.

> Principals should seek equilibrium in their leadership and avoid extremes of panic or complacency. By addressing challenges with perspective and foresight, leaders can make measured decisions that guide their schools toward enduring success.

Recognizing blind spots

The mirage of stability on the horizon

The horizon approach can create a deceptive sense of calm, making distant storms appear less threatening and peaceful waters seem enduring. Similarly, school principals can become complacent and overlook underlying issues because the immediate view seems problem-free. By examining daily operations closely, school leaders can identify and address potential challenges before they escalate, ensuring genuine stability rather than temporary calm.

The lull of calm waters

While composure is a leadership strength, some moments call for passion and energy. Principals who equate stability with effective leadership may miss opportunities to inspire their community. At times, a surge of enthusiasm—like a wave breaking calm waters—can galvanize action. For example, advocating for an inclusivity initiative requires neutrality and visible passion to engage staff and students effectively.

The illusion of proximity

The horizon can give the impression that some goals are within easy reach while others are too far to be attainable. This perspective can lead leaders to misjudge their strategic planning, as they may set excessively ambitious goals without considering the necessary small steps to reach them. They might also overlook upcoming issues because they appear too distant to require immediate action. Leaders should recalibrate their sense of scale and recognize that every objective and challenge has an actual distance that requires thoughtful navigation, much like the horizon.

Imbalance between the broad and the specific

Focusing on the horizon can prevent principals from missing essential details. Neglecting small but impactful matters can disrupt school life, while minor improvements can have outsized effects. Successful leadership requires staying alert to an imbalance between the broad view and attention to detail.

> The horizon-inspired approach encourages principals to lead with a clear, balanced perspective. By understanding the nuance of what lies beyond the visible, they prepare to address challenges and seize opportunities with vision and intention.

Reflective prompts

The horizon of stability: Embracing the calm and the storm

- How can the horizon remind me to maintain consistent leadership during times of calm and chaos?
- How do I stay composed when navigating unexpected challenges or successes?

The horizon perspective helps principals anchor their leadership, offering stability and continuity amid the fluctuating dynamics of school life.

Horizon leadership: Gaining a balanced view

- How does focusing on the horizon help me view successes and setbacks as part of a broader leadership journey?

- How can I balance emotional responses to the inevitable highs and lows of school leadership?

This perspective encourages school leaders to view successes and setbacks with equanimity, recognizing them as opportunities for learning and development.

The horizon of reflection: Using distance to gain insight
- How does the horizon inspire me to step back and gain a more expansive view of my leadership?
- How can the horizon guide me to consider both the immediate and long-term impacts of my actions?

Principals can benefit from examining their actions and policies from multiple perspectives.

Through these reflections, principals strengthen their ability to maintain a balanced perspective. They view every challenge and success as an opportunity to learn and grow, guiding their school with the calm assurance and the broad vision that the horizon inspires.

Summary

Just like a navigator uses the horizon as a guide, principals can use the horizon perspective to approach daily challenges and successes with a balanced mindset. This approach helps principals lead with calmness, patience, and foresight, recognizing that the ups and downs are all part of the bigger picture. The horizon approach is a reminder that situations are not as extreme as they may initially appear, encouraging principals to maintain a balanced perspective and not overreact to success and setbacks.

This helps prevent becoming too complacent in success or too despondent in failure, leading to a more adaptable and grounded leadership style. Principals who adopt this perspective understand that leadership is an ongoing journey. It requires a blend of long-term vision and present-moment awareness, enabling them to steer their schools with clarity and purpose. By staying composed in the face of challenges, they can make thoughtful decisions that inspire trust and confidence.

Leading with a horizon perspective is about guiding the school community through an ever-changing landscape with steady hands and a hopeful outlook. It's about recognizing that the true art of leadership lies in balancing optimism with realism, vision with adaptability, and the big picture with the small, meaningful details.

Chapter 14

The chisel and the mallet: Sculpting a vision

Picture a skilled sculptor standing before a large block of marble in an artist's studio. The scent of fresh, damp stone fills the air. As a metaphor, the block of marble represents the untapped potential of the school. It can become anything that the principal and staff can envision. With a confident motion, the sculptor begins to chip away at the first piece of marble. Although small and barely noticeable, this action marks the beginning of something significant—the initial step toward bringing to life a vision that only the sculptor can see.

The process of creating a statue from a block of marble requires vision, skill, patience, and the ability to see potential where others may see only unformed stone. Just as a sculptor slowly reveals the beauty hidden within the marble, a principal must craft a vision that shows the potential within the school, transforming it into a cohesive and thriving learning environment.

Before a sculptor even picks up their tools, they must have a vision of the final piece. They need to look at the raw marble and see the form beneath the surface, waiting to be revealed. For a principal, this initial stage involves imagining the school's potential—what it could become if given the proper guidance, resources, and opportunities. The principal must reflect on the school's values, strengths, and challenges and envision how the school can grow to meet the needs of its students, staff, and community.

In her book *Student-centered Leadership*, educational leadership expert Viviane Robinson emphasizes that effective principals are those who not only create a vision but also establish trust and encourage a culture of high expectations and constant improvement. They do this by actively involving teachers, students, and parents in decision-making and refining the vision. This process ensures that each change contributes to the realization of the vision, similar to an artist perfecting their masterpiece.

In this stage, the principal asks big-picture questions: "What do we want our school to be known for?" and "How can we best serve our students in a changing world?" The principal needs a clear idea of the desired outcome before they can begin to shape the details. This vision becomes the foundation on which every decision and action is based.

Sculpting a vision for the school requires foresight, collaboration, and dedication to transforming an abstract idea into a concrete, actionable plan that guides the school toward its full potential. When thoughtfully sculpted, a principal's vision becomes the foundation on which a thriving, successful school is built.

What this looks like

Selecting the marble: Understanding school identity

A sculptor must handpick the correct type of marble, considering its texture, size, and quality. Similarly, a school principal must deeply understand the school's unique characteristics, including its current culture, demographics, resources, and challenges. This comprehensive understanding is crucial as it enables the principal to effectively harness the school's strengths and tackle its needs by sculpting its vision.

Sketching the outline: Detailed planning

The sculptor starts by sketching initial lines on the marble to outline the rough shape of the sculpture, considering the material's properties. Similarly, the principal must develop a detailed plan with clear objectives, strategies, and benchmarks to bring the school's vision to life. This planning phase is crucial as it turns the vision into practical steps. The principal should define success at each implementation stage and establish metrics to measure progress.

Gathering the tools: Identifying resources
Sculptors need the right tools to do their work—like chisels, mallets, and polishing instruments. A principal must also gather the right tools to bring the school's vision to life. These tools include material resources, such as technology and curricula, as well as human resources, such as the skills and expertise of the staff. The principal must also consider professional development to equip teachers or enhance their capacity to support the vision.

Preparing the studio: Creating a supportive environment
A principal must prepare the school environment like a sculptor prepares their studio to facilitate a smooth sculpting process. This entails cultivating a culture that is receptive to change, where both staff and students feel empowered and encouraged to contribute to the vision. The principal should maintain regular communication on the progress of the vision, recognize minor achievements, and make necessary adaptations based on feedback from the school community.

> Crafting a vision and preparing to bring it to life in school leadership requires a delicate balance of inspiration and practical planning. As the visionary sculptor, the principal must imagine a future and carefully plan and prepare for its realization, selecting the right tools and creating an environment conducive to transformation.

Recognizing blind spots

Focusing too broadly: Losing sight of the details
A sculptor begins with a broad image of the final piece of art, but if they focus only on the overall form and neglect the finer details, the piece may need more nuance and precision to bring it to life. Similarly, a principal might become so focused on the overarching vision—big goals like improving

academic outcomes or fostering innovation—that they lose sight of the small, day-to-day elements essential to achieving those goals. Principals must balance the big-picture vision with attention to the specific, actionable details that bring it to life.

Misjudging the marble: Overlooking school readiness

When envisioning a school's future, it's essential to not underestimate the school's preparedness for change. Just as a sculptor carefully examines a block of marble before carving, a principal should thoroughly assess the school's existing culture and capabilities. Overlooking these crucial aspects could result in setting unrealistic or irrelevant goals, ultimately leading to failure or mediocrity.

Overlooking the tools: Inadequate resource planning

A sculptor's vision falters without the proper tools, and a principal's vision can do the same without sufficient resources. Initiatives lacking the necessary support, such as professional development, funding, or materials, are unlikely to succeed. Principals must anticipate and secure these resources to align the school's capabilities with its aspirations.

Sketching alone: Limited collaboration

While a sculptor may work alone, a principal's success depends on collaboration. Developing a vision in isolation risks overlooking key insights and losing essential support from staff and the community. Engaging stakeholders ensures the vision reflects shared goals and strengthens collective ownership of the school's direction.

Neglecting incremental steps: Focusing only on the end result

A sculptor shapes their masterpieces step by step, and principals must adopt the same mindset. Focusing exclusively on the end result risks ignoring the importance of incremental progress and milestones. Celebrating small wins along the way sustains motivation and reinforces commitment to the broader vision.

By addressing these potential blind spots, principals can craft a vision that is as practical as it is inspiring. Principals who attend to these details and involve their community create a vision that is clear, achievable, and deeply rooted in the needs and aspirations of their school.

Reflective prompts

Envisioning the masterpiece
- Can I clearly see and articulate the future we want for our school over the next three to five years?
- Does the vision align with the school community's core values, or is it overly influenced by personal vision?

Like a sculptor visualizing a finished work, a principal must start with a clear, community-grounded vision that reflects shared values and aspirations.

Assessing the marble
- What elements of our school's history and culture should be preserved or transformed in the new vision?
- How will the changes proposed in the vision impact the daily lives of students, teachers, and staff?

Understanding the school's foundation is essential to shaping a vision that respects tradition while improving everyday experiences.

Roughing out the shape
- Have I identified key goals that align with our shared values and will drive meaningful progress?
- Am I focusing on broad, impactful priorities rather than getting bogged down in minor details too soon?

Principals must set overarching goals that will set the stage for transformative change.

Collaborating on the sketch
- Am I actively involving all stakeholders—teachers, students, staff, and parents—in refining the vision?
- How can I ensure the vision is inclusive and reflects diverse perspectives from the entire school community?

Collaboration enriches the vision, ensuring it resonates with and represents the whole school.

Assessing the strikes of the chisel
- Am I regularly evaluating our progress toward the vision and identifying areas for adjustment?
- How do I measure the vision's success in terms of outcomes like student achievement and school culture?

Principals, like sculptors, must step back periodically to evaluate their work, ensuring alignment and responsiveness to evolving needs.

> By using these reflective prompts, principals can shape a vision that is aspirational yet grounded, inclusive yet decisive, and transformative yet achievable. This process ensures the vision remains a living, evolving guide that leads the school toward its full potential.

Summary

As a sculptor envisions a future masterpiece within a stone, a principal sees the school not as it is but as it could be—a vibrant centre of learning, innovation, and community. The process begins with a clear and detailed vision of what the school can become under thoughtful and intentional guidance.

Will it become an outstanding school and a focal point for the community, or will it stay unpolished and not fully utilized? A school leader's first step, similar to that of a sculptor, is to comprehend the material they are working with—the unique culture, challenges, and potential the school represents. The school's final shape and purpose depend on the leadership it receives.

CHAPTER 14

As a sculptor of the school's future, the principal leads the journey of vision, precision, and artistry. It involves understanding the material, applying the right tools and techniques, and being dedicated to the craft. It requires a deep understanding of the school's potential and a commitment to methodically and patiently uncovering it.

PART 3

Relational Leadership

Chapter 15

The investment fund: Relationship management

A principal's role is much like that of a banker. While a banker oversees financial transactions, a principal tends to "relationship accounts," investing in trust, maintaining open communication, and ensuring that staff, students, and parents feel valued and supported.

Positive relationships are the principal's most valuable currency, and each positive interaction—whether through active listening, honouring commitments, or providing support—serve as a deposit into these accounts. Conversely, neglecting promises, communicating inconsistently, or having a lack of transparency depletes the relationship bank account and potentially destabilizes the school environment.

Investing in these relationship accounts is essential for effective leadership. Positive interactions increase teacher satisfaction, student engagement, and school performance. Without regular investments in these relationships, conflicts can escalate, morale can decline, and progress on initiatives may falter. Principals must continually invest in their relationships to maintain a cohesive and thriving learning environment.

Investments in relationships create a reservoir of goodwill, providing a buffer against inevitable challenges. When staff feel valued through praise, support, and growth opportunities, they are more open to feedback and collaborative efforts. However, not all deposits carry the same weight, and not all withdrawals are immediately apparent. A seemingly minor action, like providing constructive feedback to a staff member, might provoke an unexpected backlash, revealing that the relationship was less secure than assumed. These complexities stem from the personal histories, sensitivities, and expectations of each individual. What one person views as helpful, another might perceive as criticism. Similarly, a policy change intended to improve efficiency could be seen as a personal slight by those most affected by it.

This dynamic underscores the importance of tailoring leadership to individual needs. A one-size-fits-all approach rarely works. Principals should understand the unique motivations and concerns of their staff, students, and parents and adjust their interactions to meet those needs. Personalized recognition, tailored professional development, and individualized support can build trust and strengthen relationships.

Maintaining these relationships requires consistent effort, even when they seem strong. Regular check-ins, genuine expressions of appreciation, and proactive communication help ensure that trust remains robust. These ongoing investments make it possible to withstand and recover from challenges, creating a school environment where relationships are strong enough to support both immediate needs and long-term goals.

What this looks like

Constant presence: The daily balance check

Managing relationship bank accounts requires consistent effort. A principal who is frequently seen in hallways, classrooms, and at school events fosters approachability and engagement. This presence reassures the school community of the principal's commitment and creates opportunities for spontaneous interactions that strengthen relationships. Everyday moments become valuable deposits in the relationship bank accounts of staff, students, and parents.

Transparent communication: Clear statements

Transparent, honest, and timely communication builds trust within the school community. Principals who provide regular updates, explain decisions openly, and offer opportunities for discussion reduce uncertainty and strengthen relationships. This transparency reassures stakeholders, just like a banker offering clear account statements, making each interaction a positive deposit into the principal's relationship accounts.

Recognition of achievements: Depositing praise

Celebrating achievements is a vital relationship-building practice. Principals who take the time to acknowledge the efforts and successes of staff, students, and parents enhance their relationships. Whether praising individuals at meetings, highlighting student accomplishments in newsletters, or honouring community contributions at events, each act of recognition adds value and appreciation, much like adding funds to a bank account.

Empathy and support: Emotional loans

Empathy and tangible support during challenging times significantly impact relationships. Whether addressing a personal crisis or a broader school challenge, principals who demonstrate understanding and provide assistance build enduring positive relations. Like a banker offering a loan during tough times, these acts of compassion strengthen relationships, ensuring they remain strong in times of adversity.

> Principals who invest in these relationships foster a motivated school community united in working toward shared goals. The ripple effect of these investments strengthens the entire school environment, ensuring collective success.

Recognizing blind spots

Inconsistent actions: Unreliable transactions

One significant obstacle for principals is inconsistency between words and actions. Relations can deteriorate when a principal's actions don't align with their commitments. Just as a banker must deliver on promised returns, a principal must ensure their actions reflect their stated values and goals. Advocating for open communication while being unavailable or promising support without follow-through damages relationships and credibility.

Overlooking small interactions: Hidden fees

While major initiatives matter, small, everyday interactions often impact relationships the most. Neglecting simple gestures, like a smile, a greeting, or a note of appreciation, is akin to accruing hidden fees that slowly deplete a bank account. These small moments are critical deposits in the relationship account, and ignoring them can leave the account overdrawn before the principal realizes it.

Failing to address conflict: Accruing interest on disputes

It's essential to be aware of the potential pitfalls of avoiding conflict. If a principal doesn't effectively deal with disagreements among staff, students, or parents, they can escalate over time, like ignoring a growing debt. Principals should proactively identify disputes early on, promote open communication, and work toward finding solutions to mend and strengthen relationships. This approach is essential for stopping unresolved issues from eroding the school's relational foundation.

Neglecting personal bias: Skewed account balances

Whether conscious or unconscious, personal biases can lead to unfair treatment and skewed decision-making. Principals must remain impartial. Self-awareness and seeking feedback are crucial to ensuring the fair and equitable treatment of all school community members. Favouritism, even if unintended, can cause resentment and damage relations.

Overreliance on formal communication: Missing informal deposits

Formal communication is essential, but relying on it exclusively can be a blind spot. While newsletters, emails, and meetings are important, casual, personal interactions are equally critical. A principal who neglects informal touchpoints misses opportunities for genuine connection. Engaging in informal conversations and being approachable in casual settings fosters stronger, more positive relationships.

By recognizing and addressing these blind spots, principals can nurture meaningful connections within their school community. Wise investing in the effort to build and maintain relationships results in a thriving and cohesive school environment.

Reflective prompts

Deposit consistency: Am I making regular contributions?
- How often do I acknowledge and praise the efforts of staff, students, and parents?
- Can I identify any patterns or gaps in my contributions?

Frequent praise and recognition are essential for maintaining healthy relationship bank accounts. Reflecting on consistency ensures principals are actively nurturing these relationships.

Withdrawal awareness: Am I minimizing unnecessary withdrawals?
- Have I made decisions recently that might be perceived as withdrawals?
- How do I balance necessary but potentially damaging actions with positive interactions?

Being aware of potential withdrawals helps principals minimize their impact, even when making challenging decisions.

Emergency fund: Am I prepared for relational crises?
- How do I handle unexpected relational crises or conflicts within the school community?
- What can I learn from a recent crisis about my approach and its impact?

Being prepared for relational challenges ensures trust is maintained during difficult times. Reflecting on past responses helps improve future crisis management.

> Engaging in this reflective practice allows principals to manage their relationships effectively, fostering a supportive and thriving school community. Like a banker evaluating investments, principals must consistently assess their relational strategies to ensure positive and enduring connections.

Summary

The relationship bank account concept highlights the importance of principals investing in relationships with staff, students, and parents. Research shows that principals who build relationships and mutual respect see higher teacher satisfaction, greater student engagement, and improved school performance. Like a banker managing accounts, principals must balance praise and support to maintain strong relationships.

Personalized interactions are key. Understanding what motivates and concerns individuals, recognizing achievements, creating professional development opportunities, and offering support when needed all contribute to healthy relationships. At the same time, principals should avoid pitfalls such as inconsistent actions, neglecting small interactions, unresolved conflicts, personal biases, and overreliance on formal communication.

By consistently nurturing these relationships and reflecting on them, principals can better navigate the challenges of leadership. Tracking interactions and their impact creates a more cohesive and positive leadership style, much like well-managed financial accounts foster stability and growth.

Chapter 16

Climbing the peak: The importance of a trusted base camp

A principal's role in school leadership can be compared to an experienced mountaineer taking on a challenging ascent. An essential aspect of this journey involves building a solid base camp—a network of trusted colleagues who offer support and guidance. Like a climber's base camp, this network is vital for success in ascending the demanding terrain of school leadership.

An essential function of the base camp is to promote open discussion, allowing principals to voice their concerns and share experiences without fear of judgment. Principals need to discuss their struggles, seek advice, and explore solutions to the complex issues they face every day. This feedback, similar to climbers debating the best approach to a challenging ascent, can be constructive for refining leadership strategies and making well-informed decisions.

Just as base camp members bring diverse skills and knowledge to support the climber, each member of a principal's trusted group should offer a unique perspective and expertise. The varied experiences of colleagues serve as a resource for handling the diverse challenges principals face. If the principal's base camp includes only like-minded members with similar leadership experiences, confirmation bias can quickly occur.

Climbers rely on their base camp to fortify them physically and mentally as they prepare to tackle the next leg of their ascent. Similarly, a principal's trusted group provides a source of resilience during demanding times. In moments of stress or self-doubt, they offer emotional support and practical strategies for overcoming obstacles. This foundation enables the principal to face difficult decisions and unexpected setbacks with renewed strength and focus.

A climber relies on their base camp team to offer honest feedback on their progress and performance, ensuring that each step is safe and strategic. Similarly, a principal's trusted group serves as a sounding board, providing candid feedback on leadership decisions and practices. This feedback allows the principal to reflect on their practices and make constructive changes, promoting growth and alignment with their leadership goals. The accountability provided by this group ensures that each "step" is purposeful, avoiding potential pitfalls on the journey. In this way, a principal's base camp becomes an essential part of their journey—offering the strength to keep climbing and the wisdom to reach new heights in school leadership.

What this looks like

Charting the course: Navigating policy changes

Educational policies are constantly changing. Like a skilled mountaineer tackling unpredictable terrain, a principal must stay informed about these changes and implement them effectively. When new policies are introduced, it is helpful for a principal to rely on a team of trusted colleagues to provide varying perspectives on implementation.

Weathering storms: Crisis management

The base camp provides vital support during crises—whether unexpected budget cuts or a global pandemic. When unfamiliar challenges occur, collective brainstorming can help develop action plans, reduce isolation, and foster connection, particularly for principals in single-administrator schools.

Checking the ropes: Embracing accountability

Principals who lead with a base camp approach value accountability. They seek honest conversations with trusted colleagues who challenge them to stay true to their goals and values. This accountability keeps the principal's leadership grounded and responsive, promoting intentional leadership growth aligned with the school community's needs.

Supporting the climb: Emotional anchors

For a principal, the responsibilities of leadership can sometimes feel overwhelming. Having a solid support system is crucial. It's not just about having a professional network; it's also about having a safe space where principals can openly share their vulnerabilities, seek guidance, and find genuine camaraderie.

> Base camp leadership empowers principals by fostering a foundation of trust and shared purpose. With the support of their network, principals navigate challenges, confront obstacles with resilience, and reach new heights in their leadership journey, knowing they have a team ready to guide them and celebrate each step forward.

Recognizing blind spots

Avoiding stagnation: Being vigilant to alternate paths

Overreliance on the base camp may lead to a lack of diverse viewpoints, similar to climbers always taking the same familiar path without considering new or safer routes. Principals should actively seek fresh perspectives to avoid the stagnation of ideas.

Overlooking the valley: Broader stakeholder insights

Principals who rely only on the insights of their base camp may need to pay more attention to insights from the wider school community. This is like a climber fixating solely on the immediate trail and ignoring critical environmental cues. Involving a broader range of perspectives can result in a more thorough approach to decision-making.

Sounds in the canyon: Echo chamber effect
To prevent echo chambers in the base camp, actively fostering debate and discussion is essential. By promoting open communication, the group can engage with diverse perspectives, ensuring that beliefs are not merely reinforced but thoughtfully examined. This approach encourages exploration and growth while enhancing overall decision-making.

Solo climbing: Ensuring independence
While the base camp provides vital support, overdependence can hinder a principal's ability to make independent decisions. Balancing the group's guidance with self-reliance helps principals build confidence in their judgment and act decisively when needed, even without immediate input.

A balanced approach to base camp leadership uses the strengths of a trusted network while remaining receptive to diverse perspectives, promoting independence and staying attuned to the wider school community. This balance enables principals to lead with confidence, adaptability, and clarity, ensuring their journey aligns with their distinct vision and the school's success.

Reflective prompts

Checking the anchor
- How often do I engage with my base camp for support or collaboration?
- How can I ensure consistent, meaningful interactions?

Regular engagement with your network fosters a steady flow of advice and collaboration, which is essential for effective leadership.

Strengthening the ropes
- How have I supported others in my base camp?
- What more can I do to empower and uplift others?

Active contributions enhance the network's resilience and strengthen its collective impact.

Guiding with a compass
- How have my base camp relationships influenced my leadership?
- Can I identify specific examples where their insights shaped my actions?

Recognizing the value of your network reinforces its importance and encourages deeper engagement.

Preparing for future ascents
- How can I leverage my base camp to address future challenges?
- How well does my base camp reflect my core values and leadership vision?

Leveraging your base camp for future challenges ensures you are prepared and supported in your ongoing leadership journey.

> By reflecting on these questions, principals can cultivate a stronger, more effective base camp. This foundation prepares them to navigate challenges with confidence and foster meaningful change within their schools.

Summary

Embracing a base camp approach to leadership offers principals a powerful framework for navigating the complex journey of school leadership. Just as a mountain climber relies on a base camp for rest, guidance, and resilience, a principal's trusted group of colleagues serves as a foundation of support, enabling them to confront challenges, refine their strategies, and maintain alignment with their school's goals.

This network fosters encouragement, accountability, and diverse perspectives. It provides a safe space for vulnerability and constructive critique, all essential for effective leadership. By seeking honest feedback and maintaining open communication, principals can address blind spots, enhance self-awareness, and align decisions with immediate needs and long-term objectives. The base camp mindset ensures principals are supported by the insights of others while retaining autonomy in their decision-making, enabling a leadership style that is both resilient and adaptable.

By balancing the insights of trusted colleagues with their own intuition and long-term goals, principals harness their interconnected leadership to create a meaningful, lasting impact. In school leadership, success is not just about reaching the highest peak alone; it involves a shared journey with a trusted team.

Chapter 17

Building bridges: Connecting people, resources, and ideas

Bridges are among our most purposeful structures. They span rivers, valleys, and divides, creating pathways where none previously existed. A bridge connects two sides that were once disconnected, allowing for the free flow of people, goods, and ideas. In many ways, a principal's role is that of a bridge builder—identifying gaps, forging connections, and ensuring that the structures they create can endure over time. Whether linking people, resources, or ideas, a principal's leadership brings together the elements that make a school thrive.

A school is a dynamic network of relationships, systems, and goals, but without attention, it can become fragmented. Teachers may work in silos, unaware of their colleagues' innovative practices. Parents might feel detached from the school's vision or unsure how to support their children's learning. Resources may be unevenly distributed, leaving gaps for students needing support. As a bridge builder, the principal identifies these disconnects and creates pathways to unite them.

The first step in building bridges is identifying any gaps, which requires keen observation and tough questions: Who feels excluded from decision-making? What resources are lacking? Where do communication breakdowns occur? Answering these questions helps the principal map their school's "disconnected terrain."

For example, a principal might observe a lack of collaboration among grade-level teachers, leading to inconsistent instructional approaches. They might also see that social-emotional services are under-resourced, leaving students without support. Identifying these gaps ensures that bridge-building efforts address the school's most pressing needs.

Bridges facilitate the flow of goods; principals must ensure the flow of resources—materials, funding, or expertise—is directed where most needed. Acting as a conduit, principals identify resource surpluses and deficits, ensuring equitable support across the school.

Bridges also connect ideas. When shared, ideas hold transformative power. As bridge builders, principals foster idea exchange by connecting the school community with professional development opportunities, outside experts, and collaboration forums. Connecting diverse perspectives ensures ideas flow freely and translate into meaningful action.

As a bridge builder, the principal recognizes the transformative power of connection. By uniting people, resources, and ideas, they replace isolation with collaboration, foster trust over division, and ensure opportunities flow to those who need them most.

What this looks like

Anticipating future gaps: Building bridges before they're needed

A forward-thinking school leader recognizes gaps before they become problems. An engineer should build a bridge to prepare for anticipated growth or shifting needs the same way a principal should proactively address potential disconnects. For example, if a school is implementing new technology, a principal might anticipate the need for teacher training and create a professional development program ahead of the rollout. This approach prevents crises, ensuring the school community is prepared to adapt and thrive.

Connecting ideas to action: Aligning vision with implementation

Bridges don't just connect two sides; they also create a pathway for movement. Similarly, a principal's leadership must bridge the gap between the school's vision and the daily realities of implementation. Ensuring that big ideas translate into actionable strategies is critical to bridge-building leadership.

CHAPTER 17

Rebuilding and reinforcing weak bridges
Not all bridges are built perfectly the first time, and even well-constructed bridges may weaken over time. Effective principals are willing to revisit and strengthen connections that have faltered, ensuring they remain resilient under changing conditions. This means regularly evaluating existing systems and relationships to identify weaknesses. It also means intentionally reinforcing connections, demonstrating a commitment to growth and improvement.

Innovating bridges for new challenges
In a constantly evolving educational landscape, principals must embrace innovation in their leadership strategies. This means exploring new ways to connect people, resources, and ideas that go beyond traditional approaches. School leadership should stay informed about emerging tools, technologies, and practices that can enhance connection and collaboration. They experiment with innovative approaches and adapt them to the unique needs of the school.

> Bridge-building leadership is not a one-size-fits-all approach—it is dynamic, adaptive, and deeply rooted in the needs of the school community. As a bridge builder, the principal becomes a unifying force, ensuring that people, resources, and ideas flow freely and purposefully. Effective school leaders maintain these connections and actively create new pathways that enable their schools to thrive in an ever-changing landscape.

Recognizing blind spots

Focusing too much on the bridge, not enough on the destination
Principals sometimes place too much emphasis on building connections without considering whether those connections serve a meaningful purpose. Bridges are tools to achieve a greater goal—they are not the goal themselves. Principals should always ask, "What is the purpose of this connection?" and align every bridge-building effort with the school's overarching mission and goals.

Underestimating the load a bridge can bear

Bridges have limits, and so do the people, systems, and processes in a school. Principals who focus on building multiple connections at once may overextend staff, resources, or themselves, leading to burnout and diminishing the effectiveness of those efforts. For example, introducing too many initiatives in one year can overwhelm teachers and dilute the focus. Prioritizing fewer high-impact initiatives ensures that bridges are sturdy and sustainable.

Neglecting bridge maintenance

Once a bridge is built, it requires ongoing maintenance to remain strong and functional. A principal may assume that a successful initiative or relationship will continue to thrive without further attention, but to ensure that, they should create systems for sustaining and revisiting connections over time. This could include scheduled follow-ups, regular feedback loops, or revising initiatives to ensure they remain relevant. Treating maintenance as an ongoing responsibility strengthens bridges and prevents them from deteriorating.

Building bridges in the wrong direction

Sometimes, principals focus on connections that seem important but do not align with the school's priorities. For example, they might invest time in creating a new partnership with an external organization while neglecting internal communication challenges among staff. Principals should align their bridge-building efforts with the school's strategic goals. Regularly revisiting the school's mission and consulting with stakeholders helps ensure that connections are purposeful and effective.

Allowing the bridge to become a bottleneck

A bridge facilitates movement but can become a bottleneck that slows progress if poorly managed. Principals should ensure that bridges are designed to empower others rather than create dependency. Delegating authority, providing clear guidelines, and trusting others to take ownership are key to avoiding bottlenecks.

An effective leader connects in ways that serve the greater good of the school community. When principals approach bridge-building with awareness and intentionality, they create pathways for supporting growth, equity, and resilience.

Reflective prompts

Surveying the terrain: Identifying the gaps
- Have I taken the time to identify the key areas of disconnection within my school?
- Am I actively seeking input from diverse stakeholders to understand their perspectives and challenges?

A bridge builder surveys the land before constructing a bridge; principals must identify the most critical gaps to effectively direct their efforts.

Blueprinting the structure: Designing for purpose
- Are the systems and initiatives I've created aligned with the school's mission and goals?
- Have I clearly communicated the purpose of these initiatives and expected outcomes to all stakeholders?

School leaders should ensure that their efforts are intentional and clearly communicated so stakeholders understand how the connections being built contribute to the school's vision.

Ensuring flow: Managing resources and opportunities
- Am I effectively identifying and addressing inequities in resource distribution across my school?
- Do I have systems in place to ensure that resources and opportunities reach the areas where they are needed most?

Equity in school leadership means ensuring that resources flow where they're needed most. Principals who lead with intention close inequity gaps and strengthen the entire school community.

Maintaining the bridge: Sustaining connections
- Am I regularly revisiting and assessing the effectiveness of the systems and relationships I've built?
- Do I proactively address emerging gaps or tensions before they grow into larger issues?

Bridges require maintenance to remain strong and functional. Principals should continuously evaluate their connections to ensure their efforts remain relevant and impactful.

> Bridge-building leadership is an ongoing journey of creating and maintaining meaningful connections within the school community. These reflections strengthen existing bridges and guide the construction of new ones, ensuring that the school remains united, collaborative, and forward-moving.

Summary

For a school leader, building bridges is transformational. By intentionally identifying gaps, creating pathways, and sustaining relationships, principals act as the architects of unity within their schools. The bridges they build don't merely span divides; they create opportunities for collaboration, innovation, and growth. These connections form the foundation of a thriving school community, where trust is built, resources flow equitably, and every stakeholder feels valued and included.

A bridge builder understands that their work is never done. Relationships require ongoing care, and the structures they create must evolve with the community's changing needs. Each bridge becomes a testament to the principal's commitment to fostering a cohesive and resilient school culture. These bridges are not just functional—they inspire trust, create opportunities, and empower everyone to cross into a brighter, more connected future.

Chapter 18

Anchoring assurance: The safety net of trust

Imagine asking the members of a school community to walk a tightrope without a safety net. Every step they take would fill them with anxiety and the fear of falling. Now, imagine that same tightrope but with a sturdy safety net underneath. With this support, steps become more assured, movements more fluid, and there is an increased willingness to take calculated risks. For school leaders, trust in a principal's leadership is the essential safety net for the school community. It underpins every action, decision, and interaction, providing the assurance and confidence the school community needs to move toward their preferred future.

Trust provides the foundation for a school culture where students, teachers, and staff can innovate, make mistakes, and grow without fear of failure. When trust is present, individuals feel supported, knowing their principal will catch them when they fall and help guide them back to stability.

Trust in the principal's leadership is a cohesive force that can unite the school community. Without trust, staff members may not feel connected to their work, and parents may wonder about the quality of the school's learning environment. A school with high trust can be more efficient and effective in its operation and management. When the school community trusts the principal's leadership, there is less room for debate and behaviour that undermine it.

Without trust, the safety net that typically supports and secures the school community disappears. When teachers, students, and parents do not trust their principal, they withhold their honest opinions and suggestions, leaving the principal unaware of the actual issues within the school.

Instead of working together toward common goals, members of the school community focus on self-preservation. This environment makes leadership an uphill battle, where every decision faces resistance and every initiative is undermined.

Parents who lack trust in their principal may withdraw their support and engagement. If they perceive the principal as unreliable or unresponsive, they are less likely to participate in school activities or support school initiatives. However, when parents trust their school leader, they are more likely to be actively involved in school life and support the school's initiatives.

When trust is woven tightly into a school's fabric, it becomes the safety net that allows everyone to push themselves to their fullest potential, knowing that they are supported and valued. Cultivating this trust is not just a leadership skill for a principal; it is the cornerstone of creating a thriving school community.

What this looks like

Strengthening the ropes: Building relationships to fortify trust

Trust is built through meaningful relationships. Like weaving sturdy ropes into a safety net, principals create trust by forging genuine, empathetic connections with teachers, students, staff, and parents. This involves active engagement, attentive listening, and sincere care for the well-being of others. Strong relationships form the backbone of a high-trust environment, ensuring the school community can withstand challenges and thrive together.

Mending the net: Repairing trust when it's broken

Even the strongest trust can fray under strain. When trust is compromised—through missteps, miscommunication, or unmet expectations—principals must act swiftly to repair it. This requires humility, acknowledging mistakes, and taking concrete steps to rebuild confidence. Offering sincere apologies and demonstrating accountability are vital for restoring trust. Like mending a torn net, repairing trust takes time, care, and a commitment to regain the school community's confidence.

Trust as the foundation of school culture

A thriving school culture relies on trust as its foundation. Principals establish this trust through consistent actions, clear communication, and a demonstrated commitment to fairness and support. When trust is ingrained in the school's culture, it becomes an invisible safety net that empowers teachers to innovate, students to take risks, and staff to collaborate openly. Parents and the broader community gain confidence in the school's direction, enabling the entire school to progress with security and shared purpose.

> Trust is not built overnight, but its presence ensures resilience during challenges and creates an environment where every member of the school community feels empowered. By cultivating trust, principals provide the safety net that supports both the school's aspirations and its people, ensuring stability and growth for all.

Recognizing blind spots

Overconfidence in established trust

A principal may assume that once trust is established, it will remain strong indefinitely. This belief can lead to overconfidence, where the principal stops actively maintaining and cultivating trust. While trust can be a strong safety net, it requires ongoing effort. If a principal takes trust for granted, they may overlook subtle shifts in staff morale or school culture that erode trust over time. Principals must remember that trust is not a one-time achievement but a continuous process that requires attention and reinforcement.

Hidden weaknesses: Unseen tensions and conflicts

Every leader carries personal biases, and when they do not acknowledge them, they can make decisions that unintentionally favour certain groups over others. These biases can weaken the community's trust, like unnoticed frays in a safety net. If minor issues remain unaddressed , it may cause a rift in the trust that has been established with the members of the school community. Overlooking or dismissing these minor concerns is akin to ignoring small tears in the safety net; although they might seem insignificant, they can expand and eventually compromise the integrity of the net.

Overlooking the anchors: Neglecting foundational relationships

Trust grows through inclusive engagement. When certain groups feel left out, they become an unsecured anchor point in a net. Trust is established by including everyone equitably within the school community. However, trust should never be assumed. Assuming that trust is already present without continual nurturing is like thinking the net doesn't need regular checks. Constant attention and reinforcement are necessary to maintain its strength and reliability.

Being a reliable neighbour: Consistency and accountability

Trust doesn't stop at the school's front door—it extends into the broader community. Imagine the school as the most prominent house in a neighbourhood. Like any good neighbour, the school is responsible for building positive relationships with those around it. A good neighbour doesn't just stay inside their home; they reach out, engage in conversations, and build relationships with those living nearby. A good neighbour doesn't wait for problems to escalate before addressing them. Similarly, a school should proactively discuss any concerns with the broader community. Whether concerns are about safety, student behaviour, or the school's impact on local businesses, principals should listen and respond thoughtfully.

> The strength of a principal's leadership will be measured by the strength of the trust they've built. A well-woven net of trust supports the school community and empowers it to innovate and grow.

Reflective prompts

Inspecting the wire: Ensuring communication and transparency

- How clear and transparent is my communication with staff, students, and parents?
- Do I regularly "test the wire" by seeking feedback, and how do I respond to it?

Open, transparent communication is the primary cable supporting the trust net. Principals can build clarity and security by ensuring everyone understands decisions and their reasoning.

Testing the tension: Evaluating consistency and reliability
- Is the tension between my actions and my expressed values consistent?
- Is the school community's trust in my leadership strong enough to nurture confidence?

Consistency between actions and words reinforces the strength of the trust net, building confidence through dependability and predictability.

Checking the safety gear: Addressing challenges and setbacks
- What are the most significant "wobbles" I face in building trust, and how do I steady them?
- How do I rebuild trust after setbacks, and what lessons do these experiences offer?

Effective principals recognize that trust-building is not always linear and requires ongoing reflection and adjustment, especially after challenges or setbacks.

Adjusting the balance: Reflecting on leadership impact
- How have my leadership decisions influenced the school's trust climate this year?
- What steps can I take to strengthen and steady trust within the community?

Reflecting on the impact of decisions helps principals understand how they have either tightened or loosened the net of trust.

Ongoing reflection ensures that potential trust issues are addressed before they escalate, keeping the safety net secure and resilient. A strong network of trust empowers school leaders to navigate challenges confidently and supports the entire community as it moves forward.

Summary

Trust is the foundation of effective school leadership and it serves as a safety net that allows the entire school community to take risks, innovate, and grow. Trust creates an environment where teachers feel empowered to experiment and challenge themselves, students feel safe to take academic and personal risks, and staff collaborate openly without fear of retribution. Trust also strengthens relationships with parents and the broader community, fostering a sense of shared purpose and partnership.

However, trust is not static. It requires continual nurturing, active listening, and a commitment to fairness and transparency. By building trust, principals create the space for healthy dialogue, respectful disagreements, and mutual accountability.

Like a safety net, trust catches the community when it stumbles, allowing it to rise again stronger, more connected, and more prepared to face the future together. Trust isn't just a leadership quality—it's the essential ingredient that enables a school to grow, thrive, and succeed.

Chapter 19

Lighting the way: Empowering aspiring leaders

Imagine a relay race where each runner is carrying a torch, passing it along the course to the next runner. In school leadership, this metaphor of lighting a torch symbolizes one of the principal's core responsibilities: nurturing future leaders. The principal lights the way forward and then hands the torch to others, empowering them to carry the flame of leadership. Leadership development in schools is not about one person holding the torch indefinitely; it's a continual process of sharing responsibility, vision, and influence to keep the light of progress burning brightly.

When principals pass the torch to their staff, they signal trust and confidence in the team's ability to lead. Whether its assigning project leadership, chairing committees, or providing mentoring opportunities, this transfer of responsibility empowers staff to shine and explore new pathways. For instance, encouraging a teacher to spearhead a curriculum initiative allows that teacher to inspire fresh perspectives among peers and, in turn, support their growth as leaders. This act not only empowers the teacher, it also fosters a culture where everyone feels invited to step into leadership roles.

Creating more leaders within a school is like lighting multiple torches. It requires the right conditions, a spark to ignite the flame, and ongoing fuel to keep the light burning brightly. Aspiring leaders need access to resources and opportunities to develop their skills, and principals need to be observant to identify those who show promise and provide them with opportunities to lead.

The continual passing of the torch illustrates the intertwining of capacity-building and leadership sustainability. Developing individual skills among aspiring teacher leaders nurtures personal growth and addresses the need for distributed leadership in any school. Intentional leadership development creates a culture within the school where leadership practices are embedded into daily operations. This approach ensures that leadership is a shared responsibility that can adapt and thrive.

A principal's role in cultivating leadership within their staff is a dynamic, visible process that lights the path for everyone involved. When a principal makes leadership development an open and shared journey, they convey that they are confident in their staff's capacity to lead.

What this looks like

Illuminating the vision

Effective leadership begins with a clear, compelling vision that resonates across the school community. Principals must consistently articulate this vision in staff meetings, newsletters, and community events, ensuring it aligns with shared goals. Highlighting success stories of staff stepping into leadership roles celebrates individual achievements and reinforces the importance of developing future leaders. Public recognition of these efforts inspires others to embrace leadership opportunities, fostering a culture of growth.

Lighting the first torch

Principals set the stage by embodying strong, visionary leadership. They serve as the initial source of inspiration, confidently addressing challenges and demonstrating how leadership can ignite positive change. Principals show how leadership can create meaningful impact through actions like launching initiatives, guiding professional development, or addressing community concerns. This visible commitment establishes a foundation for others to follow and trust in their potential to lead.

Passing the torch

Creating visible opportunities for staff to take on leadership roles is essential to the development process. Principals can do this by delegating meaningful responsibilities and projects to aspiring leaders, providing practical experience, and showing trust in their abilities. Establishing mentorship programs where seasoned leaders guide and support emerging ones creates a structured pathway for leadership growth and clarifies the development process. Additionally, offering and promoting participation in leadership training and workshops signals a commitment to professional development and shows that the school prioritizes cultivating its leaders.

> In a school where leadership development is continual, the principal doesn't simply pass the torch once but fosters an ongoing relay. By consistently identifying and igniting leadership potential, the principal transforms teachers, staff, and students from passive participants into active contributors, ensuring leadership becomes a self-sustaining and collaborative force that shapes the school's culture and direction.

Recognizing blind spots

Tending the flame: Helping emerging leaders burn bright, not out

A torch that burns too hot risks extinguishing itself too soon—just as an emerging leader who takes on too much too quickly may struggle with exhaustion. Principals must carefully balance leadership opportunities with an individual's capacity and readiness, ensuring that growth remains sustainable. Regular check-ins, thoughtful delegation, and intentional workload management prevent leadership fatigue, allowing emerging leaders to build confidence without unnecessary stress. Recognizing early signs of burnout—such as disengagement or frustration—helps principals adjust support before the flame dims.

Fuelling the flame: The power of constructive feedback

Failing to deliver consistent, constructive feedback is common in leadership development. Without clear guidance, aspiring leaders may feel uncertain about their progress or how to improve. Principals should offer regular, actionable feedback, celebrating successes while identifying areas for growth. Leadership coaching, encouragement, and transparent development plans act as the fuel that keeps the flame of leadership burning brightly.

Fanning the flames: Misjudging readiness for leadership

While it's important to empower teachers and staff to lead, not everyone is immediately prepared for the responsibilities that come with leadership. Some staff members may feel overwhelmed if they are given leadership roles without proper guidance, professional development, or clear expectations. A principal may believe that handing over responsibility demonstrates trust. Still, without suitable support structures in place, the pressure of leadership can feel more like a burden than an opportunity.

Balancing the light: Avoiding favouritism

Leaders who consistently choose specific individuals for leadership opportunities risk demotivating other staff members and hindering their growth. Similar to how balanced lighting can brighten an entire room, distributing leadership opportunities reasonably ensures that all staff members have the chance to develop and show their potential. Principals must prioritize fairness and transparency when selecting individuals for leadership roles, fostering an inclusive and encouraging leadership environment.

Lighting the path for all: Assuming leadership is innate

Instead of viewing leadership as an inborn talent, it's more productive to see it as a skill individuals can cultivate and hone. School leaders should understand that individuals have varying needs and timelines for their leadership development. This involves offering personalized support and opportunities to all staff, irrespective of their current skill level, and acknowledging that each person's journey in leadership development is unique.

Passing the leadership torch is a cornerstone of creating a resilient and collaborative school culture. By addressing blind spots, maintaining fairness, and providing consistent support, principals ensure that leadership opportunities empower their staff and foster growth and inclusion throughout the school community.

Reflective prompts

Kindling growth: Offering development opportunities

- What opportunities am I providing to help the staff carry the leadership torch?
- How am I ensuring these opportunities are accessible and engaging for all?

Ensuring all staff members have equal opportunities to develop their leadership skills will foster a more inclusive environment.

Illuminating responsibilities: Distributing leadership roles

- How am I distributing leadership roles and responsibilities among the staff?
- What steps am I taking to ensure I am not overburdening emerging leaders?

Delegation requires careful balance to provide meaningful experiences without overwhelming staff.

Guiding the flame: Providing effective feedback

- How often am I illuminating the path with constructive feedback?
- Are my feedback methods consistent and effective?

Constructive feedback is crucial for growth, and principals must ensure that the feedback mechanisms they use are consistent and beneficial.

Balancing the torch: Ensuring equity and fairness

- How can I distribute the leadership torch equally among the staff?
- How can I address favouritism or unconscious bias in distributing leadership opportunities?

The equitable distribution of leadership opportunities nurtures a culture of support and inclusion where staff members feel valued and seen.

Spotlighting potential: Discovering emerging leaders
- How am I passing the torch to identify emerging leaders among the staff?
- What strategies do I employ to recognize potential leaders who might not align with the traditional image of leadership?

Spotlighting potential ensures diverse talents and strengths are acknowledged and nurtured, rather than relying solely on conventional indicators.

> Principals must reflect on their leadership practices through consistent evaluation. With thoughtful adjustments made when needed, principals not only enhance their ability to lead but also ensure that the leadership torch is passed with fairness, confidence, and compassion.

Summary

Principals are the torchbearers of their school community, entrusted with the responsibility of lighting the flame of leadership in others. When principals pass this torch to their staff, they are not just transferring responsibility, they are igniting a light that will ensure the school's leadership distribution. By nurturing leadership potential, providing essential resources, and offering consistent support, principals ensure this torch burns brightly, lighting the way for the next generation of leaders.

With each torch-passing, the light of leadership intensifies, illuminating the path forward for all. This light symbolizes the collective knowledge, skills, and values passed from one leader to the next. It fosters a sense of unity, purpose, and shared vision within the school community. Each new leader brings their own leadership perspective, contributing to the ongoing growth and evolution of the school.

Chapter 20

Tuning the strings: Navigating tension

Imagine a guitar leaning against the wall in the corner of a room. It stands as an inert object until a player picks it up and begins tuning each string to the correct point of tension. This tension is where the potential for music lies. When the guitarist begins to play, the strings vibrate, and the music begins.

The principal, much like the guitarist, must skillfully navigate and tune the tension within their school, balancing between being too lax and too rigid. Each tension—whether among staff, between tradition and innovation, or within parent and student expectations—is represented by a guitar string that can either produce harmony or discord, depending on how it's managed (or tuned). Experienced principals understand that managing tension well can change discord into harmony.

Tension is as common in schools as are textbooks and laptops. It may exist between teachers and students, administration and staff, and the school and its community. It can arise from differences in values, resource disparities, or priorities. For example, consider the ongoing tension between student-centred and curriculum-centred approaches. The former addresses students' individual needs by recognizing their unique skills and learning styles; the latter focuses on delivering the curriculum and meeting standards. The tension between the two approaches isn't resolved by choosing one over the other; it is a dynamic balance that must be managed strategically.

Those who view such tension solely as a problem overlook the opportunities it presents for growth, progress, and positive change. Ignoring or suppressing tension is not only futile but counterproductive. Tension will not resolve itself. A skilled leader acknowledges tension and engages constructively to seek balance and growth. If addressed well, tension can lead to new understandings and more positive working relationships.

Principals frequently encounter tension in the diversity of perspectives and approaches among staff. Each teacher brings their own strengths, insights, and experiences to the school environment. Again, when thoughtfully managed, these differences create a rich, collaborative atmosphere that benefits the entire school. If ignored, however, they can lead to discord and fragmentation.

Collaboration encourages a balanced, adaptable approach that resonates throughout the school. If a principal thinks of tension as a point of potential energy, using the string metaphor, they can see it as an opportunity—a space where two opposing forces meet. By sitting with tension and examining it without rushing to resolve it, they create space for dialogue that may lead to sustainable solutions.

It is helpful to recognize that tension pulls people out of their comfort zones. It challenges assumptions, tests our skills, and demands growth. Tension can push leaders to learn, adapt, and evolve. Whatever the tension, the principal can embrace it as a positive force to transform potential discord into a cohesive, productive environment.

What this looks like

Listening deeply to find the right balance

A principal should begin by listening to the voices within the school community. They need to pay close attention to differing viewpoints and encourage staff, students, and parents to share their ideas, concerns, and aspirations. Listening builds trust and helps the principal understand the subtle nuances of each tension point and decide on the best approach to address it. By considering all perspectives, adjustments can be made that balance these viewpoints, showing that everyone's input is valued and integrated into the final decision.

Striking a chord: Unity and direction
Effectively managing tension helps create harmony within the school community. By navigating tensions judiciously, the principal will lead a collective effort toward shared goals. This strengthens the school's collective identity, turning challenges into opportunities for growth and improvement.

The crescendo: High-tension moments
A crescendo in music signifies a moment of intense power when all elements come together to create a profound impact. During crisis management, the entire school community watches the principal's performance. Effectively leading a school through high-tension periods can positively impact the community's trust in the leadership.

> Principals can effectively address tension within the school community by implementing strategies that lead to new understandings and growth. By leading with an ear for harmony, the principal fosters a school culture that is balanced and resilient, ready to meet challenges and celebrate successes together.

Recognizing blind spots

Over-tuning to breakage
To leverage tension for positive outcomes, principals may push school community members beyond their limits, causing stress and burnout. This can result in strained relationships or a breakdown of trust. To maintain a healthy balance, principals must recognize signs of increased anxiety, resistance, or disengagement among staff and students. Principals should understand when to apply some tension and when more slack is required.

Misinterpreting tension as a negative force

While tension can be a powerful catalyst for growth, a principal who sees it as something to be immediately "fixed" may lose sight of its productive potential. If every tension is treated as a problem, and differing opinions are discouraged rather than embraced, valuable conversations or ideas may be stifled, resulting in a lack of innovation. To avoid this blind spot, principals should recognize that some tensions are worth exploring and can be productive if allowed to unfold. Viewing tension as a source of learning rather than a problem to be immediately solved helps foster a culture of openness and innovation.

Muting diversity in pursuit of harmony

In pursuing harmony, there lies a potential risk. This may occur when the principal, to reduce tension, unintentionally stifles diverse viewpoints in favour of a more uniform approach. Instead, the principal should incorporate various perspectives and experiences to achieve genuine harmony within a school environment. Principals should be cautious of solutions that homogenize instead of celebrate diversity.

Confusing tension with conflict

Tension is sometimes mistaken for outright conflict. Tension can catalyze growth and innovation, but if tension escalates unchecked, it can lead to conflict and negatively impact the school culture. A principal should be able to differentiate between productive tension that fosters development and destructive conflict that hinders progress.

> Embracing tension as a leadership strategy is a delicate balance. Leading with this heightened awareness allows principals to create a school culture that fosters resilience, and maintains a healthy balance between individual needs and collective goals. By staying mindful of this challenge, principals can transform their schools into an environment where tension is embraced as a pathway to growth, connection, and lasting success.

CHAPTER 20

Reflective prompts

Striking the right chord: Assessing tension levels
- How do I determine the right level of tension for effective leadership?
- What signs indicate that staff tension is becoming counterproductive?

Identifying these signs is crucial for preventing the adverse effects of excessive stress. It is like noticing when a guitar string is too tight and at risk of snapping.

Harmonizing efforts: Balancing rigour and freedom
- How can I balance the need for structure with the freedom of creative expression among my staff and students?
- In which situations have I found it challenging to maintain this balance, and what lessons have I learned from those experiences?

Reflecting on these challenges can provide insights into more effective strategies for future situations, enhancing a principal's ability to manage tension creatively.

Celebrating harmonious notes: Recognizing effort and success
- What practices do I use to recognize and celebrate successes arising from well-managed tension?
- How can I make these recognition practices more inclusive and meaningful for all school members?

Celebrating successes reinforces positive behaviour, highlights the benefits of effectively managing tension, and fosters a culture of recognition and continual improvement.

Resonating leadership: Reflecting on personal impact
- How do my reactions to stressful situations influence the overall tension within the school?
- What strategies can I implement to ensure that my handling of tension positively influences school culture?

Developing effective strategies for managing responses can help cultivate a more positive and resilient school environment.

> Principals tune into the dynamics of their school. Regularly assessing how tension impacts the school ensures the principal's leadership promotes a harmonious and productive learning environment.

Summary

Principals should remain attuned to their school's changing dynamics. The beauty of this process lies in its ongoing nature; there is always room for refinement for better harmony. Principals should strive to embrace tension not as a barrier but as a vital force that, when skillfully managed, can drive innovation, resilience, and excellence.

In this delicate tuning, principals don't just manage tension, they transform it. Each adjustment, every decision to tighten or loosen, is an opportunity to enhance the school's overall "melody." By making tension management visible, inviting feedback, and fostering an open dialogue and an environment of continual improvement, the principal creates a culture where everyone understands their role in the collective harmony.

The most memorable melodies are not those without tension but those where someone has expertly resolved tension into something beautiful. Principals who embrace tension with empathy and intention create a school culture where differing ideas and challenges are not seen as obstacles but as catalysts for growth. They also foster an environment where staff and students feel supported, empowered, and valued.

Chapter 21

Diplomatic relations: The principal as peacekeeper

Imagine a peacekeeper in a volatile environment, diligently mediating conflicts, building bridges, and creating a harmonious community. This peacekeeper is an unbiased observer and an active force for change, addressing underlying issues and fostering a culture of mutual respect and collaboration. In educational leadership, principals often play a similar role.

Like a peacekeeper, a principal must carefully navigate a school community's complex, ever-shifting dynamics. The role of a peacekeeper is not just about resolving conflicts but also about fostering an environment where collaboration, trust, and understanding can thrive. Peacekeepers anticipate tension, acknowledge it when it arises, and work to create a culture where everyone feels heard and valued.

The work of a peacekeeper also involves balancing competing needs and perspectives. A school community is filled with diverse voices—teachers, students, parents, and staff—all with their own unique priorities and challenges. The peacekeeping principal skillfully navigates these tensions, striving for equity in their decisions while also maintaining the collective well-being of the school. The peacekeeper seeks to find common ground when there's conflict, whether over resources, workload, or educational priorities, guiding the community toward a solution that honours everyone's input without sacrificing fairness.

As peacekeepers, principals must be skilled in listening—truly listening. They must listen not only to the words being spoken but also to what is left unsaid, tuning into the emotional undercurrents that flow beneath the surface of daily interactions. Through attentive listening, they create space for reflection and understanding, helping to uncover the root of the issue rather than simply addressing the symptoms.

Peacekeeping principals recognize that a peaceful school environment isn't one where tension never occurs but one where there are systems in place to address tension constructively when it does arise. This might involve creating protocols for handling disagreements, offering regular opportunities for staff to voice concerns, or establishing restorative practices for students. These preventive measures are like the foundations of a bridge—they provide stability and strength long before anyone needs to cross.

Peacekeeping principals are bridge builders, nurturing relationships that form the foundation of a thriving school community. Their steady, compassionate leadership ensures that peace is more than the absence of conflict; it's the presence of justice, respect, and connection for all.

What this looks like

Diplomatic visibility

As peacekeepers, principals approach conflicts by fostering resolution rather than imposing solutions. For example, when two teachers disagree over instructional methods, the principal facilitates open dialogue where both sides are heard. By identifying shared goals and encouraging respectful conversation, the principal helps them find common ground, which benefits both the individuals and the broader school community. This calm, equitable mediation builds trust, showing staff that conflicts can strengthen relationships rather than fracture them.

Balancing empathy with accountability

Peacekeeping principals blend empathy with clear expectations, guiding individuals toward growth and accountability. When a mistake occurs, they listen to the personal context behind the action, offering a second chance as part of a structured path to redemption. By setting clear expectations, providing support, and ensuring regular check-ins, principals ensure forgiveness isn't seen as leniency but as an opportunity for meaningful personal growth and improvement.

Building bridges for sustained change

Peacekeepers create systems for lasting harmony. Principals use second chances as opportunities to drive long-term cultural change, making it clear that every individual's journey contributes to the school's collective growth. This approach ingrains values of trust and transformation into the school's fabric, emphasizing that mistakes are stepping stones toward a stronger, more inclusive community.

> In practice, peacekeeping principals engage in ongoing conversations with staff and students, not just during conflicts but in the everyday rhythms of school life. These informal check-ins help principals stay attuned to the community's needs and aspirations, ensuring their leadership fosters a thriving, collaborative, and resilient school environment.

Recognizing blind spots

Avoiding conflict at all costs

While peacekeepers prioritize harmony, doing so can sometimes translate into avoiding difficult conversations or making decisions that may upset the balance in the short term. For example, a principal may hesitate to address an underperforming teacher or a problematic school policy because they fear disrupting the peace. This avoidance can allow issues to fester, ultimately creating more tension and conflict over time. Effective peacekeepers must recognize that conflict, when approached constructively, is a necessary part of growth and progress.

Over-prioritizing consensus

Seeking to ensure that all voices are heard and all perspectives considered, a peacekeeping principal may delay critical decisions, creating frustration among staff who need clear direction. For instance, during a school-wide policy change, a peacekeeping principal might spend too much time seeking unanimous agreement, causing delays in implementation and uncertainty across the school. While building consensus is essential, peacekeeping leaders must also recognize when decisive action is necessary, even if not everyone agrees.

Perceived lack of strength

A calm, diplomatic approach may be misinterpreted as passivity or a lack of authority. During a crisis, efforts to mediate can be seen as indecision. To counter this, peacekeeping principals must demonstrate strength and resolve when making tough decisions, ensuring their leadership inspires confidence while maintaining fairness.

Overlooking power imbalances

In striving to create an environment of fairness and inclusion, a principal may unintentionally equate all voices as having the same level of influence or authority. However, certain groups—such as students, newer teachers, or marginalized staff—may not feel as empowered to speak up, even in a culture of openness. If a peacekeeping principal assumes that everyone has equal input without addressing these power dynamics, they risk reinforcing the very inequalities they aim to dismantle. Peacekeepers must remain vigilant in recognizing these imbalances and actively work to elevate the voices of those who may feel silenced.

Neglecting the need for urgency

Focusing on calm and balance can lead to underestimating the importance of swift action in urgent situations. Whether addressing safety concerns or student crises, peacekeeping principals must recognize when immediate action is required and ensure their measured approach doesn't hinder critical responses.

> A genuinely effective peacekeeper fosters calm and collaboration but also knows when to step into discomfort, make tough decisions, and confront challenges head-on. With this balance, the principal as peacekeeper can create a lasting, positive impact on the school culture while maintaining fairness, justice, and peace.

CHAPTER 21

Reflective prompts

Avoiding conflict or promoting growth?

- Am I avoiding necessary conversations or decisions to maintain harmony?
- When was the last time I engaged in a difficult conversation, and how did I handle it?

Avoiding conflict may seem like a way to maintain peace, but it can allow issues to fester, creating greater challenges over time. Peacekeeping principals take the time to reflect on whether their approach to conflict fosters resolution and growth.

Balancing consensus with decisiveness

- Do I delay decisions to seek full consensus, even when a timely decision is needed?
- How do I determine when to prioritize consensus-building versus making a decisive choice?

While consensus is valuable, overemphasizing it can slow progress. A desire for agreement may cause unnecessary delays and get in the way of balancing collaboration with clear leadership.

Embracing productive conflict

- Do I stifle conflict too quickly, preventing others from fully expressing their concerns?
- How can I create space for constructive conflict that leads to understanding and growth?

Conflict, when well managed, can drive innovation and stronger relationships. Before moving toward resolution, principals should consider whether they are allowing enough room for productive dialogue.

Managing calmness without complacency

- How do I convey urgency when needed without sacrificing my calm demeanour?

- In what situations could my calmness be misinterpreted as disengagement, and how can I more effectively demonstrate my commitment?

While calm leadership fosters stability, it can sometimes appear as complacency. Calmness needs to be balanced with visible urgency to reassure and motivate the school community.

> Peacekeeping leadership goes beyond resolving conflict; it creates a culture of inclusivity, growth, and mutual respect. By regularly reflecting on these aspects, principals can refine their approach to foster an empowered, thriving school environment where all voices are valued and challenges are embraced as opportunities for progress.

Summary

At its core, peacekeeping leadership is about fostering an environment where collaboration, respect, and inclusion are prioritized, ensuring that the school remains a place where all individuals—students, staff, and parents—feel heard, valued, and supported.

A peacekeeping principal cultivates harmony not by avoiding conflict but by engaging with it constructively. They understand that conflict is a natural part of any community and can be a source of growth if managed with care. Their ability to remain calm in the face of tension provides stability, reassuring their school community that solutions can be found and peace restored even during difficult times.

Peacekeeping principals build bridges, nurture growth, and create a culture of trust that empowers everyone in the school to thrive. Their leadership lays the foundation for a peaceful yet dynamic learning environment where challenges are met with resilience, conflicts are transformed into opportunities for connection, and every member of the community feels a deep sense of belonging.

Chapter 22

The juggler's skill: Humour and humility

Picture a juggler performing onstage, keeping multiple balls in the air. Each ball represents a responsibility: student achievement, professional development, school safety, community engagement—the many tasks a principal juggles daily. The juggler is serious about their craft and knows that dropping even one ball could cause the performance to fail. But while the juggler focuses intently on the performance, they also display lightheartedness. The juggler understands something essential: while the act requires focus and skill, taking the performance too seriously would make it less enjoyable for the audience.

Principals are responsible for approaching their role with seriousness, as they significantly impact the lives of students, staff, and the wider school community. But it's important to avoid taking it *too* seriously, as that can lead to rigidity, stress, and a disconnect from the people the principal is meant to inspire and lead.

The key to successful juggling is finding a balance between discipline and playfulness. Jugglers dedicate themselves to relentless practice to perfect their skills for flawless performances, and they learn to let go of fear and embrace the joy of the moment when on stage. In the same way, a principal should lead the school responsibly while feeling comfortable exhibiting human qualities, such as laughing, showing vulnerability, and connecting with others on a personal level in their day-to-day interactions. For principals, this means knowing when to be serious and when it's okay to have a lighter approach. It means using humour to make things less tense, being humble to gain trust, and staying calm when things get stressful.

A study in the *Journal of Educational Administration* supports this leadership style, showing that principals with high emotional intelligence build stronger relationships with their staff and create a more positive school climate. By not taking themselves too seriously, they model for the school community that leadership, while demanding, can also be full of joy and connection.

Of course, this balancing act isn't always easy. The demands on a principal's time and energy are immense, and the pressure to maintain high standards can sometimes make it challenging to stay lighthearted. It's essential for a principal to acknowledge these challenges, and giving themselves permission to not be perfect is essential. Remember, even the best jugglers drop a ball now and then. What matters is how they pick it up and keep going.

What this looks like

Juggling engagement: Connecting through humour and warmth

A principal who embraces this leadership style often walks the halls with a smile, stops to chat with students and staff, and uses humour to break the ice. This visible joy in their role makes them more relatable and approachable. It conveys that while their work is serious, there's always room for play and connection. This kind of engagement is more than just about being present—it's being present in a way that makes people feel at ease, humanizing their leadership.

Juggling presence: Balancing authority with playfulness

A principal who balances their authority with playfulness is like a juggler who winks at the audience while never missing a beat. They make their presence felt, but it's not heavy or overbearing. This playful approach doesn't undermine their authority; it enhances it. It shows that the principal is confident enough in their role to relax and enjoy the experience, and demonstrates to the entire community that leadership doesn't have to be rigid or stern to be effective.

CHAPTER 22

Balanced juggling: Strengthening the school community

Staff, students, and parents feel more connected to a principal who can manage serious responsibilities while remaining approachable and easygoing. The principal builds trust by effectively managing the school while still engaging with the community in a genuine, human way. A principal who models resilience through humour and joy sets the tone for how others in the school respond to difficulties. In turn, the school takes learning and work seriously but also creates an environment of laughter, connection, and shared experiences.

Embracing imperfection: Modelling authenticity

Just as a juggler occasionally drops a ball but continues with a smile, a principal who leads with humility embraces imperfection and models authenticity. When they make a small mistake or face a challenging situation, they handle it with humour rather than defensiveness, showing that they, too, are human. By acknowledging these small errors with humility, the principal conveys that perfection isn't expected; what matters is learning, growth, and connection.

> Through small, everyday gestures of friendliness, authenticity in moments of imperfection, and creative celebrations of success, this approach to leadership makes school a place of connection and growth.

Recognizing blind spots

Assuming an accurate perception

The potential exists for staff, students, or parents to perceive a principal's lightheartedness as a lack of seriousness or commitment to the job, diminishing their confidence in the school leadership. While it's essential to maintain a positive and approachable demeanour, it's equally important to demonstrate that serious issues will be addressed with the appropriate level of attention and care.

Over-focusing on applause

A juggler might focus on the applause and excitement of the audience; a principal may prioritize positive interactions over confronting serious issues. This avoidance can result in unresolved problems that may escalate over time. Principals should give equal priority to making difficult decisions to demonstrate their ability to balance lighthearted leadership with the serious work of leading a school.

The perils of improvisation

School leaders who pride themselves on being easygoing and humorous might inadvertently enforce school policies inconsistently. This can lead to confusion and perceptions of favouritism among staff and students. Principals should be consistent and fair in their application of rules and policies. They should communicate clearly about the expectations and consequences, ensuring that everyone understands that while the atmosphere can be lighthearted, the standards are non-negotiable.

The juggler's charm

While being approachable and relatable is crucial, overemphasizing these characteristics is risky. The principal may become too familiar with staff and students, potentially blurring professional boundaries. The juggler's charm can sometimes overshadow the need for authority and respect, leading to staff or students not taking the principal's directives seriously. Principals must find a balance between being friendly and maintaining a professional distance when necessary so that staff or students respect their leadership.

> By being aware of these challenges, principals can lead confidently and authentically, fostering an environment where humour and humility strengthen relationships without compromising their authority or commitment to school-wide goals.

Reflective prompts

Juggling perceptions: How am I being seen?
- Am I balancing lightheartedness with the seriousness my leadership requires?
- Do staff see me as committed and caring or overly concerned with being liked?

Reflecting on perceptions ensures your relatability doesn't undermine your credibility as a leader.

Juggling intentionality: Addressing serious issues thoughtfully
- Do I handle persistent challenges with the focus they deserve, even when lightening the mood with humour?
- Do staff and students trust that serious issues will be addressed thoroughly?

Balancing levity with intentional action ensures humour doesn't distract from resolving real concerns.

Juggling communication: Am I being clear and consistent?
- Am I clear and consistent in enforcing policies, even when being playful?
- Do staff and students understand expectations, regardless of my approachability?

Clarity and fairness in communication help maintain order while fostering a positive school culture.

> Reflecting on your approach can help you maintain balance between seriousness and lightheartedness. Regular reflection can help principals ensure they take their work seriously without taking themselves too seriously.

Summary

Leading a school is much like the art of juggling—balancing various responsibilities while keeping everything in motion. Just as a skilled juggler captivates the audience with precision and ease, a principal who combines authority with warmth and seriousness with joy can lead their school community more effectively.

This approach reminds the school community that leadership doesn't have to be inflexible to be effective. Principals who embrace their imperfections, laugh at themselves, and find joy in small moments model a growth mindset and show that it's possible to approach serious work with an open heart. This perspective invites others to adopt the same balance of resilience and openness, encouraging a school culture that values learning from mistakes, celebrating successes, and supporting one another through challenges.

PART 4

Instructional Leadership

Chapter 23

Strategic leadership: The principal as Chief Learning Officer

For years, principals have been encouraged to embrace the "Lead Learner" identity, positioning themselves as role models in lifelong learning. Although this approach has effectively promoted a culture of learning in schools, principals today may benefit from reimagining their roles to align more closely with that of a Chief Learning Officer (CLO) in a corporation. While the term "Lead Learner" emphasizes the significance of continuous learning in school leadership, it may be too limited to fully encapsulate the principal's role in fostering an environment that optimizes student learning.

The Lead Learner model emphasizes personal dedication to learning, inspiring staff by example, and cultivating a culture of growth. However, this may not fully address the systemic leadership required to implement sustainable, school-wide learning structures. A principal who is seen only as a learner may inspire but might not necessarily drive the strategic alignment of learning initiatives with broader school goals.

The CLO model broadens this perspective, focusing on the school's collective capacity. A principal in the CLO role not only models learning but also develops systems and processes that support learning for all—students, teachers, staff, and even parents. This strategic focus ensures that learning initiatives align with the school's mission and advance student outcomes.

In corporate settings, a CLO focuses on aligning all learning initiatives with the company's strategic objectives, ensuring that every program and resource supports the broader mission. Similarly, a principal as CLO leads with a strategic vision for how learning initiatives can meet the specific needs of their school. This means identifying which professional development opportunities, instructional strategies, and resources are most effective in advancing the school's goals and enhancing student outcomes.

Redefining the principal's role from Lead Learner to CLO empowers the principal to create a learning ecosystem that strategically supports staff growth, aligns with the school's mission, and adapts to evolving educational demands. As a CLO, the principal doesn't merely participate in learning but orchestrates a comprehensive approach to professional development, fostering an environment where continual growth, shared purpose, and the voices of those they lead are central to shaping the vision for professional learning.

What this looks like

Strategic alignment and vision

As the school's CLO, the principal develops a strategic vision for professional development directly tied to the school's goals. This vision goes beyond broad objectives like "improving student outcomes" by addressing specific needs such as literacy, technology integration, or student engagement. Principals ensure staff buy-in and focus by clearly communicating how these initiatives align with the school's mission and district objectives.

Talent development programs

CLOs prioritize staff growth through comprehensive professional development programs encouraging collaboration, mentorship, and tailored career plans. By customizing learning opportunities to align with individual and school goals, principals demonstrate their commitment to nurturing staff potential.

Data-driven decision-making

CLOs base decisions on data, regularly analyzing metrics like student performance and staff engagement to identify trends and opportunities. Transparent communication of this data builds trust and ensures the school community understands the direction and goals.

Continuous improvement culture
Principals can create a culture of continuous learning and improvement by implementing frameworks that empower staff to try new teaching methods and initiatives without fear of failure. This helps nurture a school environment that values adaptation. Recognizing and celebrating small victories and incremental successes creates a space where progress is acknowledged and appreciated.

Partnerships and resource optimization
CLOs understand the importance of collaborating with local businesses, universities, non-profits, and other educational organizations to combine resources and offer students exceptional learning opportunities. These partnerships help students relate their education to real-world scenarios, preparing them for future careers and citizenship.

Branding and storytelling
Crafting a compelling narrative about the school's learning culture and accomplishments helps build pride and connection within the school community. Principals should consistently share this narrative across platforms to strengthen the school's brand.

> By adopting the mindset of a CLO, principals expand their strategic vision and focus on shaping a dynamic learning environment for all school community members.

Recognizing blind spots

Data myopia
Focusing too narrowly on metrics like assessment scores can provide an incomplete picture of a school's well-being. While quantitative data is essential, CLOs must also consider qualitative insights, such as staff and student well-being and the overall school climate. A balanced approach ensures academic success is paired with social-emotional health and a positive environment.

Talent management bottlenecks
Overreliance on star performers or long-established teams can lead to bottlenecks, overworking key individuals and neglecting others. CLOs should offer diverse opportunities for all staff to develop new skills and transfer knowledge. Broadening the talent pool fosters growth and ensures sustainability.

Organizational silos
When departments or teams work in isolation, inefficiencies and a fragmented culture can result. CLOs must actively dismantle these silos by promoting collaboration, knowledge sharing, and integrated problem-solving. Accessing collective wisdom creates a more cohesive and effective school community.

Change resistance
Schools often cling to entrenched traditions, creating resistance to innovation. Principals who adhere rigidly to these practices may stifle experimentation and adaptation. To encourage growth and adaptability, CLOs should foster a culture of measured risk-taking, support pilot programs, and align successful initiatives with the school's vision.

Vision drift
Daily demands and external pressures can cause principals to lose sight of their strategic vision, weakening alignment and effectiveness. CLOs should regularly review and update their strategic plans to keep the school focused on its mission and goals.

> Recognizing these potential blind spots is essential for principals transitioning from Lead Learner to CLO. By reflecting on their practices and addressing these challenges, CLOs can create a balanced, strategic approach to professional development that fosters a thriving, engaged school community.

Reflective prompts

Strategic vision and alignment

- How well does the school's current vision align with stakeholder expectations and district goals?
- How can I refine the vision to remain relevant and inspiring?

Regular reflection ensures the vision resonates with stakeholders and provides clear direction.

Data-driven decision-making

- Am I consistently analyzing relevant data to guide critical decisions?
- Do staff understand and use data to enhance teaching and learning?

Evaluating data practices helps validate decisions and pinpoint areas for improvement.

Continuous improvement culture

- How do I encourage a growth mindset for staff members?
- How can I better support continuous improvement across the school community?

Reflecting on innovation and adaptability fosters a culture of growth and improvement.

Resource management and optimization

- Do our resource allocations align with strategic priorities, and where can adjustments maximize impact?
- How can I maximize existing resources?

Optimizing resources ensures funding, staff, and time directly support the school's mission.

> Reflecting on these open-ended questions enables principals to critically evaluate their strategies as CLOs. This reflective practice improves their capacity to create a flexible, data-driven innovative learning environment.

Summary

The shift from the concept of Lead Learner to that of Chief Learning Officer represents a significant expansion of the principal's traditional role. Principals should still commit to continually developing themselves as Lead Learners, setting a positive example for both staff and students. This model is based on the idea that principals who engage in ongoing learning contribute to creating a school culture that values growth and development.

When principals redefine their role from Lead Learner to CLO, they actively design and manage systems that foster continuous improvement, align learning with the school's mission, and empower staff at all stages of their careers. Just as a CLO in a corporation drives employee growth to support organizational goals, a principal as a CLO fosters professional development that enhances teaching quality, student outcomes, and the overall school climate.

Chapter 24

Nurturing collaboration: A thriving school garden

A school can be likened to a flourishing garden, where diverse plants grow in harmony, each contributing to the health and beauty of the whole. Tall trees provide shade, flowers add bursts of colour, and shrubs fill the gaps, creating a balanced and interconnected ecosystem. This metaphor mirrors the cooperative structures within a school, where every teacher, staff member, and student plays a vital role in the community's success. At the heart of this ecosystem is the principal—the gardener—who nurtures growth, fosters collaboration, and creates the conditions for all to thrive.

A healthy school culture, like a garden, does not emerge by chance. It requires vision, care, and an understanding of how to support each member of the community in growing to their full potential. Collaboration is more than simply assembling teams; it fosters meaningful connections and shared purpose over time. It requires cultivating relationships and a shared vision while promoting the free exchange of ideas and expertise. This dynamic interplay strengthens the school community, much like biodiversity enriches a garden, making it more resilient and vibrant.

Strategic planting is essential. In a garden, seeds must be placed where they can receive the light, space, and nutrients they need to grow. In a school, this translates to creating structured opportunities for collaboration, such as professional learning communities, cross-disciplinary teams, or grade-level groups. Like a gardener, a principal must carefully consider where and how to establish these opportunities to ensure they take root and thrive.

Challenges are inevitable, just as weeds are unavoidable in a garden. Addressing barriers to collaboration—whether through resolving conflicts, facilitating difficult conversations, or reevaluating ineffective practices—is as crucial as removing weeds from a garden. This "weeding" ensures that the healthiest and most beneficial ideas have the space to grow and flourish.

Finally, gardeners celebrate the harvest, taking pride in the fruits of their labour. In a school, celebrating collaborative successes is equally important. Recognizing achievements—whether big or small—reinforces the value of teamwork and motivates the community to continue to work together.

A thriving school culture is like a well-tended garden—rich, diverse, and resilient. Through thoughtful planning, intentional care, and continual attention, principals can cultivate a collaborative environment where everyone feels valued and empowered to contribute. A principal who approaches leadership with a gardener's mindset—thoughtful, patient, willing to get their hands dirty—creates a school where collaboration is not just a practice but a way of being.

What this looks like

Cultivating relationships and trust

In every garden, a plant's growth is influenced by its interactions with the soil, sunlight, and neighbouring plants. Similarly, a school principal reinforces collaborative frameworks by nurturing connections and cultivating trust among the staff. Staff members should view the principal as a leader actively participating in cooperative structures. This dedication to building relationships is the foundation of a strong community, not unlike the strong roots of healthy garden plants.

Pruning and steering growth

A gardener prunes plants to help them grow stronger, and a collaborative principal knows when to focus the school's efforts on the most impactful initiatives. They are selective about the projects and goals they pursue, recognizing that too many initiatives can overwhelm staff and dilute the effectiveness of collaboration. The principal is thoughtful about priorities, ensuring the focus remains on what will truly benefit the school community.

Fertilizing with resources and opportunities

Just like a gardener uses fertilizer to enrich the soil and improve the garden's overall health, a principal shows leadership by enhancing the school by providing support and opportunities for professional development. When a principal advocates for funding, introduces innovative technologies, and supports initiatives for growth, the school community can see that the principal is dedicated to providing the necessities to cultivate a vibrant learning environment.

Removing weeds

In any garden, weeds can threaten the health of the plants, and a collaborative principal addresses any challenges that might disrupt a culture of teamwork. They recognize when issues arise—conflict between staff members, a lack of engagement in collaborative meetings, or an obstacle to effective communication—and take steps to resolve them with care and empathy. This could involve providing additional training, adjusting expectations, or facilitating difficult conversations to resolve conflicts. By addressing challenges directly and compassionately, the principal ensures that the "weeds" don't take over, allowing collaboration to continue to grow strong.

> A principal who leads with this mindset creates a school culture where collaboration is a daily practice—where every community member has a role in helping the school flourish. By leading as gardeners, principals ensure that the school community is productive and rooted in a common purpose.

Recognizing blind spots

Overlooking the undergrowth

Similar to how small plants might be overshadowed by larger ones in a garden, the contributions of a school's quieter teachers, students, and staff members may be overlooked by others. Failing to recognize the contributions of these quieter members stifles the potential for new ideas and perspectives that could enrich the school's collaborative efforts.

Ignoring water regulations

Overwatering or underwatering a garden can be problematic. In a school, too much control can stifle initiative, leading to dependency and inhibiting innovation. Conversely, too little guidance can leave teachers feeling lost and unable to reach their collaborative potential. Principals must regularly evaluate their involvement in collaborative processes, ensuring they offer enough support without overwhelming or neglecting their team.

Using the wrong fertilizer

A garden thrives when fertilized appropriately, but using the wrong type or amount can harm the plants. In a school, the "fertilizer" is feedback, but it must be constructive and tailored to the recipient. When feedback is too sparse or harsh, it can undermine collaborative initiatives. Effective principals cultivate a culture of positive, actionable feedback that encourages growth and improvement without causing burnout or resentment.

Failing to rotate crops

In gardening, rotating crops helps maintain soil health and prevent nutrient depletion, and in a school, rotating leadership roles and team structures can keep the collaborative culture vibrant. A principal who relies on the same people or ideas for every project may miss out on fresh perspectives and innovation. This lack of diversity can lead to a stagnant environment, where collaboration becomes routine and predictable rather than dynamic and creative. Principals should rotate team members, invite various staff to lead initiatives, and encourage experimentation with new approaches. This variety keeps the collaborative "soil" fertile, allowing new ideas to take root and ensuring the garden remains healthy and diverse.

CHAPTER 24

Pruning too early or too late

Pruning at the right time is essential for a garden's health to remove parts of plants that are diseased or inhibiting growth. In school leadership, this translates to addressing issues as they arise, whether performance-related, behavioural, or structural. Principals who act too hastily may cut off potential before it can bloom; if they wait too long, problems can grow and spread. Striking the right time for interventions requires careful observation and understanding, much like knowing when pruning is most beneficial for a plant.

> Just like gardeners need to understand the specific conditions of their garden and adapt their practices to ensure every area flourishes, principals must become skilled at recognizing and dealing with the less obvious aspects of their leadership. By identifying these blind spots, principals can ensure that their school's collaborative environment is as lively and productive as a well-maintained garden.

Reflective prompts

Planting seeds

- Am I intentionally creating opportunities for collaboration, or am I relying on unstructured interactions to sustain teamwork?
- Do the teams established have clear goals, roles, and purposes that align with the school's vision, or are they struggling to find direction?

In a garden, planting is not haphazard but intentional, with careful attention to placement and conditions.

Are the roots receiving enough support?

- Are trust, respect, and our shared goals adequately supported and nourished?
- How can I strengthen the support systems for effective collaboration?

Healthy collaboration relies on trust, respect, and shared goals.

Is there enough light shining on every plant?
- Am I giving equitable attention and opportunities to all staff and students?
- How can I ensure every school community member is noticed and represented?

Equitable attention and opportunities are critical to inclusive and effective collaboration.

How deep are the roots?
- How deeply connected are the members of our school community?
- What can I do to strengthen the relationships and networks within our school?

Strong interconnectedness among community members fosters mutual aid and shared growth.

> By regularly asking reflective questions, principals can ensure their collaborative structures remain responsive to the school community's needs. This reflective practice is more than just a task; it's an ongoing commitment to nurturing an environment of collaboration, trust, and shared success.

Summary

Creating a collaborative school culture is much like nurturing a garden—it requires patience, intentionality, and a deep commitment to continual care. Collaboration, like a diverse and well-tended garden, leads to a more resilient and vibrant environment where different voices come together, ideas take root, and collective efforts bear fruit.

However, a thriving garden doesn't emerge without careful attention to potential challenges. Just as a gardener must weed and prune to maintain the garden's health, a principal must be willing to address conflicts, offer constructive feedback, and guide teams through difficult conversations. This openness to refinement ensures that collaboration remains strong and focused. Additionally, a collaborative culture flourishes when diversity is valued, bringing various perspectives that make the school more adaptable and creative.

A collaborative school is more than just a place of work; it is a dynamic ecosystem where each member contributes to the overall health and success of the community. It is a place where trust is cultivated, creativity is encouraged, and every voice has a chance to be heard.

Chapter 25

Measuring impact: Is the juice worth the squeeze?

Imagine a school as a thriving orchard, each tree representing a unique program or initiative that supports the learning environment. In this analogy, the principal is the orchard keeper, tasked with ensuring that the fruits—initiatives and programs—are worth the time, effort, and resources required to cultivate them. The guiding question becomes, Is the juice worth the squeeze? That is, do the benefits justify the investment?

The effort spent nurturing trees in the orchard—watering, pruning, fertilizing—must eventually produce a healthy harvest. If the trees fail to bear fruit, or if the fruit is small and bitter, the orchard owner must question whether the time and labour are justified. Similarly, principals must evaluate whether the energy, resources, and time invested in a program produce results that justify its continuation.

For instance, a professional development program focused on implementing a new digital assessment system may require significant time, planning, and resources. While the system may offer some efficiencies, the principal must ask whether these benefits justify the ongoing investment. If the gains are marginal, with teachers struggling to integrate the technology effectively or the system failing to provide meaningful insights, the principal may determine that the "juice" is not worth the "squeeze" and decide to explore other, more impactful, professional development opportunities.

School leaders must constantly weigh the outcomes of a program—whether improved student results, staff engagement, or community involvement—against the size of the investment. If a program is draining time, energy, and financial resources without delivering significant results, it may be time to reassess whether it is worth sustaining.

The principal must also consider the opportunity cost: what other initiatives could the resources support that might yield greater benefits? This requires the principal to examine a program's effectiveness and potential future impact. Does reallocating resources currently used on less impactful programs better serve emerging needs or opportunities within the school community?

Like tending to an orchard, leading a school requires constant evaluation, care, and difficult decision-making. A principal's role in evaluating the impact of programs is critical to ensuring that the school's resources are used wisely and that every initiative contributes to its long-term success. Asking "Is the juice worth the squeeze?" challenges principals to carefully assess whether the time, energy, and resources invested in a program are yielding meaningful results.

What this looks like

Planting with purpose
An orchard keeper plants trees with a clear vision of the desired harvest. Similarly, a principal sets clear goals and expectations for every program or initiative. This requires defining measurable outcomes and ensuring that the school community understands the objectives and criteria for success. For instance, when launching a student engagement program, the principal might aim to improve attendance, boost participation in extracurricular activities, or strengthen student-teacher connections. Setting purposeful goals provides clarity and ensures alignment with the school's broader mission.

Analyzing the soil
Healthy orchards depend on healthy soil, which needs to be analyzed to determine if it has the necessary nutrients. For principals, this translates to analyzing data to inform decisions. Metrics such as test scores, attendance rates, and budget allocations provide principals with the information they need to evaluate whether programs are meeting their intended goals. This

data-driven approach provides a foundation for transparent, evidence-based decisions that justify resource allocation, and demonstrates the value of critical thinking and analysis to staff and the broader community. It ensures that initiatives are grounded in reality and aligned with the school's unique context and needs.

Pruning for growth

An orchard keeper regularly prunes branches to encourage healthier growth and ensure resources are not wasted. Similarly, a principal must make tough decisions about adjusting or discontinuing initiatives that fail to deliver meaningful results. For example, if a technology program doesn't significantly enhance student learning despite considerable investment, the principal might phase it out or reallocate resources to more impactful projects. Pruning isn't about abandoning effort but redirecting energy toward initiatives that genuinely benefit the school. These decisions can be challenging, but they are essential for sustaining the overall health of the school community.

> Leading like an orchard keeper involves planting initiatives with clear intent, supporting their growth through thoughtful resource allocation, and pruning when necessary to focus on what truly matters. Principals create an environment where programs and people can thrive by fostering a culture of intentionality, adaptability, and accountability. A school led with this mindset will yield lasting benefits for students, staff, and the community.

Recognizing blind spots

Squeezing only the sweetest fruits

Confirmation bias—the tendency to seek information confirming one's beliefs—is a common challenge that decision-makers face. However, by being aware of this tendency, decision-makers can actively seek diverse perspectives and consider a broader range of information to make well-rounded decisions. It's like being open to exploring all the fruits in an orchard, recognizing that even those that may not look appealing initially could offer valuable nutrients and long-term benefits.

Missing the fruit tree for the orchard

Various factors must be considered when assessing a school's success and programs. While metrics like test scores and attendance are crucial, they paint only part of the picture. Principals should also consider qualitative factors such as student engagement, teacher morale, and the overall school environment. Effective leadership requires examining quantitative *and* qualitative data to understand what drives student success. This approach helps ensure decisions are not based solely on numbers but also considers the school culture and the feedback of the entire school community.

Chasing immediate harvests

Under pressure to produce quick results, principals may implement strategies that yield rapid gains but lack sustainability. For example, celebrating a temporary spike in student performance from a new instructional method without evaluating its long-term viability risks overlooking future challenges. Effective leadership requires a focus on sustainable practices that adapt to evolving needs, ensuring that today's gains don't become tomorrow's setbacks.

Reluctance to prune old branches

Just as an orchard keeper must be willing to remove trees that no longer bear fruit, a principal must recognize when a program no longer provides value and be prepared to make tough decisions about discontinuing it. Holding on to outdated or ineffective initiatives can drain resources and prevent the school from focusing on more promising opportunities. For example, a principal may hesitate to cut a technology initiative that has become outdated because significant time and resources have been invested in it. Failing to adapt and move on from unproductive programs can hinder the school's progress. Principals must regularly assess whether each program is still "bearing fruit" and be willing to make changes when necessary.

Leading like an orchard keeper requires principals to nurture, evaluate, and adapt programs while remaining alert to blind spots that can undermine their effectiveness. Through regular reflection and a commitment to evidence-based decision-making, principals can ensure their school grows and thrives.

Reflective prompts

Nurturing young trees: Initial implementation

- Since implementing this program, what initial outcomes or benefits have we observed?
- How has the reception been from students, teachers, and parents?

Early feedback establishes a baseline for future evaluations, helping principals ensure the program starts strong and aligns with community expectations.

Planting the right seeds: Clear goals and expectations

- Have we clearly defined what success looks like for this program?
- Does the program align with our school's mission and long-term goals, or are we pursuing something misaligned with our priorities?

Principals must clarify expectations and ensure that programs are purposefully chosen to serve the school's specific needs.

Assessing the fruit: Evaluating outcomes

- Are the results of this program proportional to the effort and resources invested?
- Does the program produce outcomes that truly benefit students and staff, or are we overly focused on superficial metrics?

Principals must critically evaluate whether programs are delivering deep and meaningful impacts.

Harvesting the best fruit: Maximizing impact
- What measurable improvements in student outcomes can be attributed to this program?
- How does this program align with our school's goals and priorities?

Principals can validate the program's impact and relevance by measuring tangible improvements and ensuring alignment with strategic goals.

Pruning for future growth: Balancing resources
- Are we overinvesting in this program at the expense of others needing attention?
- Could reallocating resources yield greater benefits elsewhere?

Resource allocation must be balanced to support a diverse and thriving "orchard" of programs, preventing overinvestment in initiatives that offer limited returns.

Harvesting lessons: Learning for the future
- What lessons can we draw from this program's successes or challenges to inform future initiatives?
- Have we gathered enough data and feedback to understand why this program succeeded or fell short?

Reflecting on successes and failures ensures that lessons learned from each program improve future planning and implementation.

> By asking thoughtful, open-ended questions, principals can gain a deeper understanding of the impact and value of their efforts. This helps to ensure that principals use resources effectively, align programs with school objectives, and involve the entire school community on a continual improvement journey.

CHAPTER 25

Summary

An orchard keeper knows to tend to trees with care, thoughtfulness, and strategic vision; an effective principal knows to nurture school programs and initiatives with the same level of attention and insight. From planting the seeds of new ideas to tending to programs as they grow and making difficult decisions about pruning those that no longer bear fruit, the principal plays a critical role in cultivating a healthy, thriving school community.

At the heart of this leadership approach is intentionality. Principals should set clear goals for each program and ensure that these goals align with the school's broader vision and values. Like selecting the right seedlings for the orchard's soil, principals must thoughtfully choose initiatives that support the school's long-term growth and success, always asking whether the "juice is worth the squeeze."

As an orchard keeper, the principal is a leader who blends vision with pragmatism and growth with discernment. This commitment to continuous reflection ensures that the school remains responsive to changing needs, adaptable to new challenges, and focused on achieving the best outcomes for students, staff, and the wider community.

Chapter 26

Tending the fields: The circle of control

Imagine a principal standing at the edge of their school, much like a farmer surveying a vast field. The principal nurtures this environment, ensuring growth, balance, and productivity.

Within this field lies the principal's circle of control—the areas where decisions, actions, and leadership directly shape outcomes. Beyond it, external forces—unexpected district policies, societal challenges, or shifting community dynamics—are outside their influence. To lead effectively, principals must learn to focus on what they can control and develop strategies to navigate what they cannot.

In a principal's circle of control are the areas they can tend with care and intentionality: the relationships they cultivate, the culture they shape, the professional growth of the staff, and the well-being of the students. A principal plants and nurtures these "crops" through their expertise, attention, and values. For instance, fostering a positive school culture creates the conditions for learning and collaboration to thrive. A principal empowers teachers to grow through clear communication and thoughtful professional development. Every decision a principal makes—every seed they sow—directly contributes to the resilience and health of the school.

But just as a farmer cannot control the weather, a principal cannot control challenges outside their influence. External policies may shift, funding may fall short, or a sudden crisis may disrupt plans. These forces can feel overwhelming, but focusing on the response is key. By recognizing what is beyond the circle of control, a principal can conserve energy for what matters most: supporting the school community and creating strategies to mitigate the impact of external challenges. For example, developing contingency plans or fostering a culture of adaptability can help the school weather unexpected storms with strength and purpose.

Leadership through the circle of control requires clarity and patience. Positive change, like a growing crop, takes time to bear fruit. Principals must balance their focus across multiple priorities; too much attention in one area risks neglecting others.

Leading within the circle of control is not about ignoring what lies beyond it; it's about focusing on where the most significant difference can be made. The way a principal chooses to lead within their circle of control has a profound and lasting impact on the health and vitality of the school. Intentional efforts will yield a stronger, more resilient community.

What this looks like

Preparing the soil: Building a strong school culture

Like farmers cultivating fertile soil to sustain growth, principals create an environment where trust, respect, and collaboration flourish. Leadership in this area requires intentionality. Principals should start by ensuring all members of the school community understand and commit to a shared vision. Conflicts or misunderstandings need to be addressed quickly to prevent them from undermining trust. A principal's influence over culture lies in demonstrating their values and building alignment with the team. This foundation ensures the school can endure external challenges while remaining focused on its goals.

Planting the seeds: Empowering staff and students

Leadership isn't just about managing; it's also about empowering others to grow. Principals, like farmers selecting seeds, must identify opportunities for staff and students to thrive. Empowerment comes from delegating meaningful responsibilities, encouraging innovation, and fostering leadership at all levels. For a principal, leading within the circle of control includes creating these opportunities and supporting them to succeed. When individuals feel valued and capable, the entire school community benefits.

Tending the crops: Providing support and resources

Sustained growth requires consistent attention. A leader ensures their team has the resources, training, and encouragement it needs to succeed. Principals can make the most significant impact within their circle of control by addressing barriers, supporting professional development, and maintaining open lines of communication. Leadership in this area requires adaptability—being present enough to recognize when additional support is needed and proactive enough to remove obstacles before they hinder progress.

Protecting from the elements: Navigating external pressures

External factors—such as policy changes, district mandates, or societal pressures—are beyond a principal's control, but how a principal responds to them is not. Strong leaders build resilience within the school to mitigate the impact of these challenges. They anticipate potential disruptions by developing contingency plans and fostering a culture of adaptability. When new mandates or policies arise, they lead with transparency: explaining the rationale behind decisions, involving the staff in problem-solving, and prioritizing actions that protect core values. They demonstrate steady, purpose-driven leadership by focusing on what they can influence—such as how the school adapts.

Harvesting the yield: Celebrating growth and success

Celebrating success is an integral part of leadership, such as acknowledging milestones both big and small, whether that is improved academic performance, the success of a staff-led initiative, or a student's personal growth. Celebrating these accomplishments builds a sense of shared purpose and momentum. The role of a leader is to shine a light on these successes, ensuring everyone feels their contributions are valued.

By focusing on what they can directly influence—supporting staff, empowering students, and nurturing a positive culture—the principal ensures a sustainable path for the school's development. At the same time, by preparing for and managing external factors, they maintain a forward-thinking approach that keeps the school flourishing, no matter what challenges arise.

Recognizing blind spots

Hidden weeds: Overlooking subtle issues

In a farmer's field, weeds can start small and spread if not detected early. For principals, blind spots often present as insignificant issues that are initially overlooked within the school. These could include minor conflicts among staff, slight signs of student disengagement, or early indications of burnout among staff members. By promptly addressing these hidden weeds, principals can prevent them from becoming more significant problems later.

Weather changes: Underestimating external influences

Monitoring weather patterns is crucial for farmers as external changes can significantly affect their crops. Similarly, principals need to be mindful of external influences that could impact their school beyond their circle of control. Policy changes, community issues, or shifts in school trends can significantly shape the school environment. By anticipating and preparing for such changes, principals can adjust their leadership approach to ensure that their school remains adaptable to external pressures.

Shaded areas: The unseen impact of indirect influence

In a farmer's field, shaded areas might affect crop growth. Similarly, principals must be aware of the indirect influences that may not be immediately visible but still impact the school environment. For instance, a principal's decisions on resource allocation or policy implementation might inadvertently affect certain student groups or staff members differently. Regularly reviewing the outcomes of decisions and seeking feedback can help principals identify these indirect impacts and adjust their strategies accordingly.

Overlooking the need for balance: Rotating the crops

In farming, planting the same crop year after year depletes the soil, just as focusing too narrowly on one area of a school's operations can exhaust resources and energy. A blind spot can develop when principals place disproportionate emphasis on one aspect of the school at the expense of others, whether it be academic performance, student behaviour, or community engagement. Principals must ensure they are rotating their focus regularly, giving adequate attention to all areas to keep the school thriving holistically.

> Like a farmer who identifies issues with their field to ensure a bountiful harvest, a principal who recognizes and manages deficiencies in their leadership is better able to foster a positive learning environment. In doing so, principals ensure that their leadership yields the best possible results for students, much like a well-tended field.

Reflective prompts

Evaluating the soil: Foundations of leadership

- Have I created an environment of trust where staff and students feel valued and supported?
- How do I assess and maintain the health of my school's culture?

Healthy soil is essential for crops to thrive, and a sound foundation within your circle of control is crucial for the well-being and success of students and staff.

Watering the crops: Providing support

- Am I proactively identifying and addressing the specific needs of staff and students within my control?
- How do I allocate resources to ensure maximum impact on the areas I can influence?

Like crops that need regular watering, staff and students require ongoing encouragement and resources to thrive.

Inspecting for pests: Addressing challenges
- How well do I prepare my school for external pressures beyond our control?
- What structures or plans have I implemented to minimize the impact of external pressures on the school community?

Farmers inspect their fields to catch and eliminate pests early; a principal must be alert to potential issues within their circle of control.

Rotating the crops: Encouraging innovation
- How am I encouraging innovation and fresh approaches in teaching and leadership?
- How do I foster a culture where staff and students value continuous learning?

A principal who encourages new ideas and practices within their circle of control ensures that the school continues to grow and evolve.

> Reflective questions are a powerful tool for principals to ensure they lead with intention and purpose. Just as a farmer regularly assesses the condition of their crops and land, principals must continuously reflect on their leadership approach to cultivate a thriving, resilient school environment.

Summary

A principal standing at the edge of their school community, much like a farmer gazing over their fields, can view the success of their leadership, which hinges on understanding and mastering their circle of control. Principals can channel their energy into actions that foster growth, innovation, and long-term success by understanding what they can control and what lies beyond their reach.

Circle-of-control leadership intentionally shapes an environment where teachers, students, and staff feel supported and empowered to contribute their best. Like the farmer preparing soil, planting seeds, and tending crops, principals who lead with clarity and purpose ensure their schools thrive from the inside out.

This approach equips the school to be more resilient and adaptable to external challenges, building a community grounded in trust, shared leadership, and collective effort. It shifts reliance away from external factors and onto the strength of what the principal has cultivated within their control. The result is a flourishing school where success is sustainable, growth is intentional, and every community member feels empowered to weather challenges and embrace opportunities.

Chapter 27

Effective leadership: Taking the pulse

In medicine, checking a patient's pulse is essential for assessing their health. Monitoring a patient's pulse can alert health care providers to important issues that require immediate attention. Similarly, a principal must regularly assess their leadership to ensure the vitality of their school community. A doctor doesn't wait for a patient to fall ill before checking for warning signs, and a principal should not wait for problems to arise before evaluating their leadership effectiveness. By taking regular "pulse checks" on their leadership practices, principals can ensure they are leading with purpose, addressing the needs of their school, and fostering an environment of growth and success.

Taking the pulse of a school community isn't just about gathering data—it's more an act of self-reflection. A principal's leadership is closely connected to the well-being and performance of their school. When they are assessing the school's health, they are also holding up a mirror to their leadership practices, decisions, and behaviour.

A critical component of leadership pulse checks is emotional intelligence—the ability to remain open, self-aware, and responsive without becoming defensive. Principals must approach feedback with curiosity rather than resistance. When staff express frustration or disengagement, effective leaders do not see it as criticism of their leadership but as an opportunity to strengthen their connection with the community. Practising deep listening, asking clarifying questions, and demonstrating a commitment to action reassures staff that their voices are valued and their concerns will be addressed.

Preventive care is crucial in medicine. By regularly monitoring a patient's health, doctors can catch warning signs early and provide treatment before conditions worsen. The same principle applies to leadership. When principals engage in regular self-assessments, they can spot potential issues before they impact the broader school culture. For example, if a principal notices through feedback that staff feel disengaged or unsupported, they can address that proactively, preventing burnout or dissatisfaction from spreading.

In their book *The Leadership Challenge,* James Kouzes and Barry Posner argue that successful leadership is not a destination but a journey characterized by a commitment to ongoing learning, receptiveness to feedback, and dedication to personal and organizational development. This philosophy aligns with the concept of "taking the pulse," portraying the leader as someone constantly pursuing improvement and attuned to the heartbeat of their school.

Effective leadership is not static; it evolves based on the needs of the people being led. By regularly assessing the school's pulse, the principal can make informed adjustments to their leadership practices. For example, if feedback reveals a dip in staff morale, it may be time to focus on team-building initiatives or revisit workload distribution. These adjustments, grounded in real-time data and community feedback, ensure that the leadership remains responsive and relevant.

What this looks like

Preparing the stethoscope: Setting clear objectives

Before taking the pulse of their school community, principals need to prepare themselves just like a doctor prepares to use a stethoscope. This means they must set clear, measurable objectives for what they hope to assess about their leadership. It involves defining the critical components of effective leadership within their specific school context. Principals should ask themselves what signs of healthy leadership they are looking for and what symptoms might indicate areas of concern they need to address.

CHAPTER 27

Finding the right pressure points: Engaging the community

Effective pulse-taking requires engaging the entire school community, including students, parents, teachers, and support staff. By gathering input from diverse voices, principals gain a comprehensive understanding of the school's climate and culture. This inclusive approach also reinforces stakeholders' sense of value in the decision-making process.

Reading the pulse: Analyzing feedback and data

Once feedback has been received, it should be carefully analyzed to develop a clear and comprehensive understanding of the current landscape. This includes identifying patterns, recognizing strengths, and pinpointing areas for growth. Principals should attend to both qualitative feedback—such as comments, conversations, and observations—and quantitative data, including survey results and performance metrics. Paying close attention to divergent viewpoints or emerging signals may reveal deeper, unaddressed issues.

Continual monitoring: Establishing a routine for pulse-taking

To fully benefit from pulse-taking, principals should make it a routine practice rather than a one-time checkup. This involves scheduling regular times to interact with stakeholders, collect feedback, and evaluate leadership methods. Continual monitoring enables principals to stay attuned to the state of their leadership and make real-time adjustments to meet the evolving needs of their school community. It also fosters a culture of transparency and ongoing improvement, ensuring that stakeholders feel their input is acknowledged and respected.

> By incorporating regular leadership assessments into their practice, principals cultivate a dynamic, healthy school environment where staff and students thrive. Effective leadership depends on ongoing reflection, adjustment, and growth.

Recognizing blind spots

The variable pulse: Inconsistent measurement methods
Inconsistent measurement methods can lead to misunderstandings about the school's actual state and the effectiveness of leadership strategies. By standardizing these methods, principals ensure they compare consistent data points, making it easier to track progress and identify changes in the pulse of their leadership.

Focusing only on quantitative data: Missing the emotional and cultural pulse
While quantitative data, such as test scores or attendance rates, is important, it doesn't capture the emotional or cultural well-being of the school. A high-performing school, on paper, might still grapple with staff burnout, student disengagement, or inclusivity challenges. Principals must also assess the school's qualitative dimensions—staff morale, the tone of daily interactions, and the sense of belonging among students. This dual approach offers a holistic view of leadership effectiveness.

The fading resonance: Complacency in successful areas
Success can breed complacency. Principals may focus on emerging issues while neglecting previously successful programs or initiatives. Without sustained attention, these areas may lose their impact over time. A balanced approach that nurtures existing strengths while addressing new challenges ensures a dynamic and thriving school environment.

The pulse echo: Confusing symptoms with cause
Understanding the distinction between symptoms and the underlying cause is essential for effective treatment in medicine. Similarly, in school leadership, principals must carefully analyze whether they are addressing the symptoms of a problem or its root cause. For instance, low student engagement could be symptomatic of deeper issues, such as inadequate classroom resources or teacher support. Principals must delve deep to identify the true causes of problems, ensuring that their interventions are impactful and sustainable.

Just as doctors must be vigilant for hidden symptoms affecting a patient's health, principals must be aware of potential blind spots. By broadening their assessment practices, principals can ensure that their leadership remains responsive, balanced, and effective.

Reflective prompts

Listening for the heartbeat: Aligning values and action

- Are my actions consistently aligned with my stated values and the school's vision?
- Have I made compromises that undermine these values, and how can I correct them?

Much like a doctor listens to a patient's heartbeat to check for irregularities, a principal needs to evaluate whether their leadership practices align with their intended direction.

Checking the pulse of the community: Listening to feedback

- How often do I seek input from staff, students, and parents about my leadership?
- Am I creating opportunities for all voices to be heard, especially those less vocal?

Principals should gather feedback from various sources to understand how their leadership is perceived.

Monitoring vital signs: Measuring outcomes and impact

- What indicators reflect the health of my leadership (e.g., staff morale, student engagement, academic performance)?
- Am I balancing quantitative data with qualitative insights to get a complete picture?

Principals should regularly assess both the hard data and the more subjective indicators of school success.

Checking the reflexes: Responding to feedback and criticism
- How do I handle constructive criticism, and how has it shaped my leadership recently?
- What specific changes have I made based on feedback to improve my leadership?

Reflecting on reactions to criticism and the subsequent changes helps principals ensure that their leadership pulse is receptive and attuned to the needs and suggestions of others.

Taking the pulse of leadership requires humility, openness, and a dedication to growth. Like a physician using a pulse check to assess health, principals can use these reflective prompts to evaluate and adjust their leadership. By doing so, they ensure their leadership remains impactful, resilient, and aligned with their school community's evolving needs and aspirations.

Summary

An engaged and vibrant school environment is like a strong and steady pulse in a patient—it's a clear indicator of good health and effective leadership. The school's "pulse" is evident in quantitative data, such as academic performance, and the more subtle qualitative feedback, like staff and student morale. Principals must finely attune themselves to these signals, recognizing that numbers and emotions tell the story of the school's well-being. By carefully monitoring this pulse, leaders can detect early signs of success or emerging challenges, allowing them to intervene promptly and keep the school community thriving.

Assessing leadership effectiveness requires active listening, deep reflection, and intentional action. Principals who master this practice enhance their leadership skills and create a responsive, nurturing school environment. Through continual assessment and thoughtful adjustments, school leaders can cultivate an atmosphere of excellence that serves the entire school community, ensuring its "heartbeat" remains strong, steady, and aligned with its mission and values.

PART 5

Operational Leadership

Chapter 28

Antivirus leadership: Safeguarding school culture

One of the most crucial responsibilities of a principal is maintaining and nurturing a positive school culture. Toxic behaviour—whether from staff, students, or parents—can undermine the health and well-being of the entire school community. Such behaviour can manifest as persistent negativity, gossip, resistance to change, bullying, lack of professionalism, or disengagement. If left unaddressed, it can erode trust, lower morale, hinder collaboration, and ultimately affect student outcomes. A principal's role in managing and mitigating toxic behaviour is central to ensuring that the school remains a safe, supportive, and thriving environment for everyone.

Like antivirus software, principals must protect the school community against harmful influences. Negative behaviour of staff members can penetrate a school's culture, disrupt harmony, and hinder the overall progress of the staff. If left unchecked, toxic behaviour can spread throughout the school like a virus, affecting morale and undermining the collective efforts of the school community. Principals must identify, isolate, and address these toxic elements to ensure a healthy school environment.

Once the causes of toxic behaviour are identified, they must be prevented from spreading. Directly addressing those exhibiting the behaviour can minimize the impact. Principals should engage in constructive conversations, offering clear feedback on specific behaviour and avoiding personal attacks. This approach creates a pathway for positive change.

This involves implementing targeted interventions and support systems. Professional development programs to enhance interpersonal skills and stricter measures when necessary can rebuild the integrity of the school's culture. Ongoing monitoring and follow-up, akin to regular system checks, ensure the complete elimination of issues and prevent residual effects.

Principals should lead by example, demonstrating the values and behaviour they expect from their staff. Consistent, fair, and compassionate leadership sets a significant precedent, influencing the overall atmosphere and culture of the school. Providing professional development opportunities that focus on positive school culture and effective communication equips staff with the tools to navigate interpersonal challenges constructively. By setting clear expectations, fostering a culture of accountability, and maintaining regular vigilance, principals can eliminate toxic behaviour before it spreads, ensuring that the school environment remains healthy, positive, and conducive to growth.

What this looks like

Running regular scans: Observing and listening to the school community

Just as antivirus software runs regular scans to detect potential threats, a principal should consistently observe the school environment and listen to feedback from staff, students, and parents. This means being present in classrooms, attending meetings, and conducting informal check-ins to gauge the school's climate. The principal can catch early signs of toxicity before it escalates by paying attention to subtle shifts in tone, energy, and relationships within the school.

Frequent updates: Consistent communication

Antivirus software needs regular updates, and principals should keep up-to-date by establishing open and consistent communication within the community. By regularly sharing responses to any feedback, principals show they take concerns seriously.

CHAPTER 28

Quarantining the problem: Addressing toxic behaviour quickly and clearly

Antivirus software quarantines potential threats to prevent them from infecting the rest of the system. Similarly, when a principal identifies toxic behaviour, they must address it quickly, clearly, and directly to ensure it does not spread. This means having one-on-one conversations with those involved, setting clear expectations, and outlining the changes that must be made. By quarantining the issue, the principal limits its impact on the broader school culture while providing a chance for resolution.

User-friendly interface: Accessible support

Principals should implement accessible support systems for staff and students. Clear outlines for seeking help and resources, such as counselling services and professional development workshops, address the underlying causes of negative behaviour and encourage growth. Clear reporting channels protect anonymity and ensure safety when reporting issues.

Building a firewall: Consistency and follow-through

Antivirus software often includes a firewall to block future threats. Similarly, a principal should establish preventive systems that make it harder for toxic behaviour to take hold. This involves building a strong school culture grounded in trust, respect, and collaboration. Implementing transparent communication channels, providing conflict-resolution training, and setting up peer support networks are all ways to create a firewall against negativity. A strong firewall helps ensure that the school culture remains resilient, even in the face of inevitable difficulties.

> By regularly scanning the school environment, quarantining issues before they spread, reinforcing positive behaviour, and providing support for change, the principal protects the integrity of the school community.

Recognizing blind spots

Hidden viruses: Subtle negative behaviour
Some computer viruses are sophisticated enough to evade detection. In a school community, subtle forms of toxic behaviour can go unnoticed even with a vigilant principal. This behaviour could include exclusion, microaggressions, or passive-aggressive actions, which may not be as easy to identify as overt issues, such as some forms of bullying. Principals should actively encourage open dialogue and provide anonymous reporting channels to highlight hidden behaviour and ensure it is addressed before it escalates and causes harm.

Invisible impacts: Underestimating consequences
Remember that toxic behaviour can have lasting effects, like a virus that causes long-term harm beyond the immediate disruption. Conducting regular climate surveys and encouraging open communication can help principals understand the broader impact of toxic behaviour. By recognizing that minor issues can escalate if addressed, principals can take steps to tackle problems early.

Inconsistent updates: Failure to reinforce expectations
Principals need to reinforce behavioural expectations consistently. Failure to do so can lead to confusion or inconsistency in managing behaviour; even well-communicated expectations can fade from focus, leading to behavioural lapses and a lack of accountability. Principals must also ensure that expectations are regularly updated and communicated to keep them relevant and top of mind.

Losing focus on the positive: Getting caught up in problem-solving
Antivirus software is designed to seek out and eliminate threats, but a principal's leadership should not be solely focused on problem-solving. Becoming fixated on addressing negative behaviour and losing sight of the positive aspects of school culture can create an environment where staff feel that problems are always prioritized over successes, leading to a culture of

negativity or criticism. Principals should strike a balance, dedicating attention to both solving problems and promoting the positive elements of the school.

> Like hidden viruses, subtle negative behaviour can undermine the health of a school community if left unchecked. Principals play a vital role as the system's vigilant protectors, ensuring that harmful patterns are not only detected but also addressed thoughtfully and proactively. The balance lies in addressing issues without losing sight of the strengths that define and uplift the school community. Effective leadership neutralizes threats, but beyond that, it cultivates a resilient and thriving culture.

Reflective prompts

Scanning for early threats: Identifying toxicity before it spreads

- Am I observing and listening to the school community to detect early signs of toxic behaviour?
- Have I created meaningful opportunities for staff and students to express concerns about the school culture, and how do I act on this feedback?

Early detection is crucial. Like running scans to catch hidden computer viruses, principals must actively engage with their school community to identify minor concerns before they escalate, fostering a healthier, more responsive environment.

Firewall settings: Establishing boundaries

- What boundaries have I set to prevent toxic behaviour from taking root or spreading?
- Am I consistently reinforcing these boundaries across all levels of the school community?

Boundaries act as a protective firewall. Reflecting on their effectiveness and consistently applying them helps principals create a safe and respectful environment for staff and students.

System maintenance: Continual improvement
- How often do I review and refine my strategies for managing toxic behaviour?
- What new tools, approaches, or insights can I integrate to address emerging challenges more effectively?

By regularly evaluating and updating their approaches, principals can stay ahead of evolving challenges and maintain a healthy school culture.

User permissions: Empowering staff
- How have I empowered staff to take an active role in addressing toxic behaviour?
- What additional training, support, or resources can I provide to make staff feel confident and capable in tackling these issues?

Empowering staff creates a collaborative culture. Principals should consider how their leadership enables teachers and other staff to address challenges proactively and confidently.

> Continual self-reflection and improvement are essential for effective school leadership, similar to how regular checkups and maintenance are crucial for keeping a computer healthy. This approach allows principals to stay vigilant and responsive, ready to address challenges and uphold the well-being of the entire school community.

Summary

Like a sophisticated antivirus system, a principal's leadership must consistently detect, manage, and prevent toxic behaviour that can undermine a school's healthy functioning. This requires a nuanced understanding of when to intervene, how to foster positive change, and what preventive measures to implement to safeguard the school's climate.

Prevention is critical to maintaining a healthy school environment. Principals can achieve this by promoting a positive culture through consistent communication, visible actions, and accessible support. This strategy also requires leading by example, treating everyone fairly, and establishing trust through consistent actions.

Antivirus leadership is about creating a school environment that is free from toxicity and thriving with positive relationships, trust, and a shared sense of purpose. Such leadership ensures the school has the tools, systems, and culture to handle challenges with grace and strength, even when challenges arise.

Chapter 29

The scales of leadership: Moving between hope and hard truths

Leading a school requires constant calibration, much like a set of scales does. On one side of the scales is realism—the weight of responsibilities, constraints, and external pressures. On the other side is optimism—the belief in growth, possibility, and the collective strength of a school community. Often, a school leader's success hinges on maintaining a balance between these two forces, ensuring that neither outweighs the other.

When realism dominates, leadership can feel heavy, marked by frustration or resignation to obstacles. If optimism overpowers, it risks becoming disconnected from reality, leading to unmet expectations and disillusionment. The most effective principals recognize that true leadership is not about choosing one over the other but about balancing the scales with intention.

Maintaining this balance means acknowledging challenges without letting them determine the future. It means leading with transparency—being honest about difficulties while reinforcing the school's capacity to navigate them. For instance, in times of crisis—a sudden budget cut, a shift in district policy, or an unexpected event in the community—a principal who leads with balanced communication might say, "This is a tough situation, and there are real challenges ahead. But we are resourceful, we are resilient, and together, we will find a way forward." This kind of leadership steadies the school, instilling confidence while keeping expectations grounded in reality.

Time constraints make this balancing act even more difficult. The demands of leadership rarely allow for lengthy reflection to recalibrate. Yet, a principal can use small but intentional moments, such as pausing to collect their thoughts before addressing staff and seeking perspectives from trusted colleagues to help maintain balance, preventing the scale from tipping too far in either direction.

Realism provides the foundation—it grounds decisions in facts, data, and a clear understanding of the school's current circumstances. Optimism is the counterweight—it lifts the vision, guiding staff and students toward a preferred future. Principals should ensure that their leadership decisions are rooted in both. For example, when setting academic goals, a principal must assess performance data realistically, ensuring that targets are attainable. But they must also frame these goals as part of a larger vision for growth, reinforcing the belief that progress is possible with sustained effort.

Leadership is not about always keeping the scales perfectly level. Challenges will arise that shift the weight in one direction or another. The key is being aware of when adjustments are needed and having the confidence to recalibrate. A principal who masters this balance creates a school environment that is both steady and forward-moving—one where obstacles are met with resilience and opportunities are embraced with hope.

What this looks like

Making micro-adjustments

A well-calibrated scale never remains perfectly still—it shifts slightly with every added weight, adjusting to maintain equilibrium. Likewise, a principal who leads with both realism and optimism must constantly recalibrate in response to new information, unexpected challenges, and evolving school dynamics. Effective leaders stay grounded in their long-term vision while making thoughtful adjustments along the way, ensuring that no single challenge tips the balance too far in one direction. Whether addressing a sudden staffing shortage, responding to shifts in student needs, or navigating district policy changes, the ability to adapt while remaining focused is key to keeping the school community moving forward.

CHAPTER 29

Remaining steady under pressure
A scale must be built strong enough to hold firm when external forces threaten to tip it, just as a principal must provide stability in times of crisis. When uncertainty arises—whether due to budget constraints, community disruptions, or a global event—a leader's composure sets the tone for the entire school. Principals who balance realism and optimism acknowledge difficulties without allowing them to create panic. Instead, they frame challenges as opportunities for problem-solving and collective resilience.

Knowing when to shift weight
Balancing the scales requires knowing when to hold steady and when to shift weight strategically. Sometimes, the moment calls for consolidation—reinforcing systems, stabilizing staff morale, or strengthening instructional practices. Other times, it requires leaning into change—introducing an initiative, taking calculated risks, or pushing the community toward growth. A skilled leader assesses the conditions and makes intentional decisions about when to pause and when to move ahead. Ignoring this balance can lead to burnout or stagnation; managing it well creates a school culture that is both stable and forward-moving.

> A principal who embraces this approach leads a school that is resilient and hopeful, grounded in present realities yet open to future possibilities. Their leadership becomes the steady force that ensures progress—one adjustment at a time—toward a thriving school community that is prepared for whatever lies ahead.

Recognizing blind spots

Overcorrecting the scales
A principal who leans too heavily toward realism risks creating an atmosphere of discouragement, where challenges dominate the narrative and possibilities feel unattainable. On the other hand, unchecked optimism can leave staff feeling unheard, as real concerns may be glossed over in favour

of an overly optimistic outlook. Effective leadership requires careful calibration—acknowledging obstacles while reinforcing a sense of agency and possibility. A principal who leads with this balance ensures that concerns are validated, but they do not define the school's trajectory. The most successful leaders make room for both realism and optimism, ensuring that neither side tips the scales too far in one direction.

Misreading challenges

A principal should develop the skill of accurately assessing the severity of challenges. Underestimating an issue—such as declining staff morale—can lead to delayed or inadequate responses, allowing it to grow into a more significant problem. Overestimating challenges, however, can create unnecessary stress, leading to reactionary decisions that disrupt stability. Leadership that is well balanced seeks diverse perspectives, consulting staff, students, and trusted colleagues to gain a clear understanding of each situation before acting. Leadership is not about reacting to every shift but rather making informed, measured adjustments to maintain equilibrium.

Rushing leadership decisions

Rushing through leadership decisions can destabilize progress. A principal eager to showcase success may push for quick fixes—implementing initiatives hastily or seeking immediate results. However, meaningful change is rarely instantaneous. Some solutions may create the illusion of progress but fail to address deeper, systemic issues. Effective principals take a measured approach, ensuring that each step forward is intentional, grounded in solid planning, and aligned with the long-term vision of the school.

Being complacent in leadership

Principals must be vigilant in recognizing that balance in leadership is not something achieved once and then set in place indefinitely. Overconfidence—assuming that a well-balanced approach will sustain itself—can lead to complacency. A principal who has successfully navigated a period of high morale cannot assume it will persist without continued effort. The dynamics of a school community are constantly evolving, and what worked yesterday may not be enough tomorrow. Effective leaders remain engaged, continually assessing and fine-tuning their approach to ensure the school remains both stable and forward-moving.

> Leading a school with both realism and optimism requires continual recalibration. The goal is not to achieve a perfect, unshifting balance; it is to develop the awareness and flexibility to adjust as needed. Effective principals recognize that leadership is dynamic, requiring attentiveness, humility, and the willingness to learn from each adjustment.

Reflective prompts

Weighing challenges and possibilities

- Am I communicating both obstacles and opportunities with clarity, or do I tend to emphasize one over the other?
- Do I frame challenges in a way that acknowledges reality while reinforcing confidence in our ability to adapt and grow?

If the scale tilts too heavily toward challenges, the weight can feel overwhelming; if it leans too far toward optimism, concerns may be dismissed. Balanced communication ensures transparency while fostering a culture of trust, resilience, and forward momentum.

Measuring the weight of challenges accurately

- Am I assessing challenges based on solid data and multiple perspectives, or am I relying on assumptions?
- Do I engage diverse voices to avoid misjudging the significance or urgency of an issue?

A well-calibrated scale detects even slight imbalances, and effective leadership requires the same precision.

Adjusting the scale of progress
- Am I pushing for quick wins at the risk of instability, or am I moving too cautiously and missing opportunities for meaningful change?
- Do my expectations and timelines promote steady, sustainable growth, or do they encourage rushing or stalling?

School leadership requires pacing—moving forward with intention while allowing time for initiatives to take root. Thoughtful adjustments ensure progress without overwhelming staff or sacrificing depth for speed.

Distributing the weight of leadership
- Am I engaging staff, students, and families as partners in decision-making, or am I carrying too much alone?
- Do I foster a culture of shared leadership where different perspectives inform and strengthen our collective work?

A balanced scale relies on even distribution. Strong principals recognize that leadership is not a solitary act; they create structures for collaboration, encourage open dialogue, and trust in the collective capacity of their school community.

> Balancing realism and optimism is not a one-time achievement. It requires ongoing adjustments, thoughtful recalibration, and the ability to respond to shifting circumstances. These questions help principals assess their leadership approach, ensuring that they remain steady, adaptable, and focused on guiding their school community forward with clarity and confidence.

Summary

Leading a school requires two carefully calibrated essential forces: realism and optimism. Similar to balancing a set of scales, the challenge lies not only in managing the weight of daily demands but also in ensuring that both truth and possibility receive their rightful consideration. A principal who leads with balance understands that hope is most potent when grounded in reality, and that challenges confronted with clarity and intention become opportunities for growth.

Mastering this balance requires discernment and adaptability. A leader who leans too heavily on reality may create a culture of hesitation, where obstacles feel insurmountable. Conversely, unchecked optimism, disconnected from the complexities of the school environment, can leave staff and students feeling unheard and unprepared. The most effective principals skillfully adjust the scales, acknowledging struggles while reinforcing the collective ability to overcome them.

Balancing realism and optimism is not about achieving a perfect equilibrium; it is about leading with intention, authenticity, and the awareness that leadership itself is a dynamic act of constant recalibration. Each challenge presents an opportunity to strengthen resilience, and each success, no matter how small, serves as proof that progress is possible. A principal who masters this balance becomes a steadying force within their community—one who anchors the present while keeping an eye on the future, ensuring that their school remains both grounded and moving forward.

Chapter 30

Choosing battles wisely: When to step in and when to step back

A principal's leadership often mirrors that of a general on the battlefield, where strategic decision-making is crucial for success. No matter how minor the conflict, a general must decide on the extent of engagement to avoid depleting resources, exhausting troops, and losing focus on the larger war. In the same way, a principal who intervenes in every small issue that arises risks diverting energy, eroding trust, and losing sight of the overarching goals of the school.

Principals need to know when to engage and when to hold back, exercising restraint in managing day-to-day challenges. The ability to discern which issues are worth addressing and which can be allowed to pass is critical to maintaining long-term stability, focus, and success in a school environment.

In a military campaign, a general's troops must feel trusted, valued, and capable of carrying out their duties without constant oversight. Micromanaging every move can undermine trust, leading to disengagement and diminished morale. The same principle applies in a school setting. Teachers and staff need to feel that their professional judgment is respected and that they are trusted to manage minor issues in their day-to-day work.

When a principal chooses to be involved in every battle—intervening in small, relatively inconsequential matters—they risk creating a culture of micromanagement and undermining staff confidence. However, just as an overly involved general risks exhausting their troops, a leader who remains too distant may leave their team feeling abandoned. Principals must strike a balance between intervention and autonomy—ensuring that while they trust their staff, they are also present and responsive when genuine guidance, mediation, or direct leadership is required. The key is not disengagement, but intentional leadership: stepping in at the right moments while allowing staff the space to lead and problem-solve independently. For example, if a teacher's slightly relaxed approach to homework policies works well for their students, intervening to enforce strict adherence to a school-wide policy might do more harm than good. The teacher may feel their professional judgment is being questioned, which could lead to frustration or resentment. Instead, by choosing not to intervene, the principal demonstrates trust in the teacher's ability to make decisions in the best interest of their students.

A principal must focus on the issues that truly matter: those that impact student well-being, school culture, or long-term goals. Addressing every minor issue can scatter attention and energy, pulling focus away from the larger, more important battles that require leadership and action.

What this looks like

Differentiating battles from problems

One of the key distinctions a principal must make as a strategic leader is recognizing whether an issue is a battle to be won or a problem to be solved. Battles imply conflict, opposition, and a clear victory or loss, while problems involve complexities that often require collaborative solutions and ongoing effort. In the context of school leadership, understanding this difference is crucial. When a principal frames an issue as a battle to be won, they often rely on their own authority to impose a solution. This can be necessary in situations where core values are at stake or when swift, firm action is needed to prevent harm. However, when faced with a problem to be solved, a principal's role shifts from authoritative decision-maker to collaborative facilitator. Problems typically require building partnerships, fostering trust, and empowering others to take ownership of solutions.

Focusing on high-impact issues

A principal who acts like a wise general prioritizes high-impact issues over minor concerns. They recognize that while minor infractions or deviations might be noticeable, not all require immediate action. If addressing these minor issues would distract from more important tasks—like implementing a school-wide mental health program or improving student literacy rates—the principal may choose to let them go. By focusing on the most significant growth areas, the principal keeps the school moving forward and avoids being sidetracked by less critical matters.

Exercising restraint

Strategic principals exercise restraint, understanding that constant intervention can lead to micromanagement and a lack of trust. This approach is built on the belief that teachers and staff are professionals capable of managing small challenges independently. By not intervening, the principal signals they trust the teacher's professional judgment, fostering a culture of independence and creativity. This hands-off approach, when appropriate, empowers staff and creates a sense of ownership over their work.

Engaging with precision

Strategic leadership involves knowing when to step in and address problems that could escalate or impact the school's overall performance. The key is balance—engaging when necessary but not intervening in every situation. For example, a principal might notice ongoing tension between two staff members that has started to affect the classroom environment, gone beyond a minor disagreement, and begun to interfere with student learning. In this case, the principal would step in to help resolve the problem and ensure it doesn't escalate further. The principal's decision to intervene is strategic, focusing on an issue that, if left unchecked, could undermine the school's success.

> A principal who leads like a general demonstrates strategic thinking, trust, and a focus on long-term success. Ultimately, strategic leadership fosters growth, development, and success for every school community member.

Recognizing blind spots

Missing the signs: Overlooking emerging problems

A principal might ignore minor issues, believing they will resolve themselves. However, some problems left unchecked can escalate, affecting morale, school culture, or student outcomes. If ignored for too long, what began as a minor concern could eventually undermine the school's standards. Principals must be vigilant by consistently reviewing emerging patterns to ensure small problems don't grow into major issues.

Potential for collateral damage: The cost of nonintervention

The potential for collateral damage exists when a principal chooses not to intervene. For example, in an attempt to preserve their relationship with teachers, the principal decides not to take action when a few teachers repeatedly bend school rules (such as grading deadlines or classroom expectations). This can set a precedent for others. Before long, the entire staff may perceive that accountability is lacking, undermining trust and leading to inconsistent standards throughout the school.

Misjudging the stakes: Underestimating the impact

Sometimes a principal may misjudge the importance of what may seem to be a minor issue because they don't fully understand the impact. By misjudging the stakes, the principal may miss an opportunity to address root causes early, allowing the issue to grow until it becomes more difficult to manage. Principals must continually evaluate both the visible signs of a problem and its underlying causes and potential long-term impact.

Overly relying on staff autonomy: Assuming issues will self-correct

While trusting teachers and staff to handle minor issues is often beneficial, there's a risk in assuming that problems will self-correct without the principal's guidance or oversight. Sometimes, staff may not feel equipped to handle specific challenges independently and might need their leader's intervention. A principal must strike a balance between empowering staff and ensuring support is provided when necessary to prevent issues from stagnating.

While choosing battles wisely can be a powerful leadership tool, it has risks. Like a skilled general, a principal must know when to fight a battle and recognize when seemingly minor issues require attention to prevent more significant consequences.

Reflective prompts

Understanding the battlefield: Identifying key priorities

- Am I focusing on the most critical issues that align with the school's long-term goals, or am I getting distracted by less important concerns?
- Are the battles I choose to engage in directly contributing to the school's mission and vision?

Addressing high-priority challenges reinforces the school's core objectives and prevents energy from being wasted on distractions.

Gauging the cost of engagement: Weighing the risks and rewards

- What are the potential costs—in time, energy, relationships—of intervening in this issue, and do the benefits outweigh these costs?
- What are the potential consequences if I choose not to engage, and am I prepared to accept them?

With every challenge, a principal must clearly understand the stakes and potential outcomes of engaging.

Knowing when to retreat: Understanding the value of nonintervention

- In what situations have I chosen not to intervene, and were those decisions ultimately beneficial for the school and its stakeholders?
- Have there been instances where nonintervention allowed staff to grow, innovate, or resolve issues independently without my involvement?

Just as a general must know when to retreat and avoid unnecessary conflict, a principal must recognize when nonintervention can lead to better outcomes.

OPERATIONAL LEADERSHIP

> Strategic leadership involves knowing when to act and understanding the broader consequences of each decision. By doing so, principals can refine their leadership and make thoughtful, impactful decisions that benefit the entire school community.

Summary

Just as a general must decide the extent of engagement in any battle, a principal must evaluate which issues are worth addressing to ensure the school's long-term success. Strategic leadership is about balancing action with restraint, knowing when to intervene and when to let minor concerns pass in favour of more pressing priorities.

At the heart of this leadership style is discernment—understanding the cost of each battle and weighing the risks and rewards of intervention. Principals ensure that their energy and resources are directed toward issues with the most significant impact by choosing battles that align with the school's mission and vision. Conversely, deciding not to engage in every minor issue preserves staff morale, empowers teachers to manage their own challenges, and prevents the principal from becoming bogged down in less critical matters.

Choosing battles wisely means maintaining focus on the big picture while still attending to the details that matter. It is about preserving relationships, fostering growth, and leading with purpose. Ultimately, it's not about fighting every fight but about engaging in those that move the school toward its broader goals.

Chapter 31

Guiding the flow: Boundary leadership

Imagine a river winding through the landscape. The river's flow is powerful, carving valleys and creating pathways through the land. Yet, this flow is only possible because the riverbank's natural boundaries contain and direct the water's movement. Leadership boundaries for principals can be likened to the banks of a river, defining the scope and limits within which a principal operates.

Without riverbanks, the water can overflow, flooding the surrounding areas and causing damage. Similarly, if a principal's boundaries erode, the flow of their leadership becomes uncontrolled, leading to burnout, inefficiency, and strained relationships.

These boundaries encompass everything from professional ethics to the limits of personal involvement, from the policies that govern a school to the unwritten rules of school culture. They define the roles, responsibilities, and personal space of every individual—teachers, staff, students, and parents. A principal who understands these boundaries is like a skilled river guide, adept at navigating the complexities of the school landscape.

Boundaries are not just about protecting time and energy; they are about sustaining leadership for the long haul. A principal who consistently overextends themselves risks exhaustion and diminishing effectiveness. However, when boundaries are intentionally maintained, leadership remains energized, sustainable, and impactful—allowing principals to guide their schools with clarity and confidence.

Maintaining the integrity of their leadership boundaries begins with self-awareness: understanding one's limits, values, and priorities. It involves setting clear expectations with the school community and communicating these boundaries consistently and respectfully. Like reinforcing riverbanks to prevent erosion, principals must regularly assess and adjust their own boundaries to ensure they remain effective. This might involve reflecting on areas where boundaries have blurred, seeking feedback from trusted colleagues, and making necessary adjustments to align with their core values and leadership goals.

When boundaries are respected, leadership flow becomes strong, purposeful, and directed. When staff, students, and parents understand the principal's boundaries, they are more likely to feel secure and supported. They know what to expect and can engage with the principal effectively and respectfully.

What this looks like

The visible bank: Consistency in action
A school leader's boundaries should include clear expectations, transparent decision-making, and fair application of rules. For example, a principal may respect teachers' autonomy to innovate while providing necessary support or establishing specific hours for availability to manage their time effectively. Predictable behaviour fosters trust, as the school community relies on the principal's steady leadership.

The flow of communication: Clarity through dialogue
Boundary leadership also requires open communication to foster understanding and buy-in. A principal might highlight the importance of work with life balance by setting an example, such as limiting responding to emails after hours. By articulating these boundaries, they encourage staff to follow suit, creating a ripple effect where personal and professional limits are respected.

CHAPTER 31

Shaping the school environment: Creating a culture of boundaries

Principals who model boundary leadership cultivate a school culture where expectations are clear and roles are respected. This might mean starting and ending meetings on time, using professional development days efficiently, and valuing personal time. Such practices foster order and mutual understanding, guiding interactions across the school community.

> Like riverbanks shaping the flow of water, strong boundaries guide leadership and positively influence the school environment. Principals create a culture of shared expectations and respect by consistently modelling and communicating their boundaries.

Recognizing blind spots

Overrigidity: The trap of inflexibility

While boundaries provide necessary structure and protection, implementing them without flexibility can lead to a leadership style that feels unyielding or disconnected from the needs of the school community. Principals must regularly reflect on whether their boundaries serve the greater good or create unnecessary barriers that discourage or alienate staff and students. The challenge lies in finding the right balance—knowing when to bend without breaking and when to adapt without compromising the integrity of their leadership.

Setting invisible boundaries: The risk of unspoken expectations

Unspoken or invisible boundaries can cause confusion and frustration within a school. A principal may assume their boundaries are understood, but if these boundaries are not communicated clearly, they remain unseen and may lead to misunderstandings and unclear expectations. This lack of clarity can erode trust and create friction within the school community. Transparency in setting and explaining boundaries helps prevent this.

Eroding boundaries: The slippery slope of overinvolvement

The gradual erosion of riverbanks can cause a river to lose course, and a principal's boundaries that weaken over time can result in them becoming too involved in areas that should be left to others. This overinvolvement, often driven by a desire to help or control outcomes, can lead to blurred lines and diminished leadership effectiveness. When a principal takes on tasks or responsibilities that should belong to others, they risk overstepping their role, which can lead to burnout and diminish the capacity of others to lead. Delegating effectively and trusting the team's capabilities are crucial to maintaining healthy boundaries.

Boundary blindness: Ignoring the boundaries of others

Principals must be aware of and respect the personal and professional boundaries of those within the school community. A principal who oversteps or ignores these boundaries—unnecessarily intruding on a teacher's autonomy, disregarding a student's privacy, or failing to respect a staff member's time—risks damaging relationships and eroding trust. Principals must remain sensitive to individual needs and limits, ensuring their leadership honours the autonomy and dignity of all school community members.

> Boundary leadership is not about rigid control but thoughtful guidance. Like a skilled navigator who understands a river's challenges, principals must balance clear direction with respect for diverse needs, steering their schools safely and effectively through the changing currents of education.

Reflective prompts

Assessing the riverbanks: Strength of boundaries

- Are my leadership boundaries strong enough to guide my responsibilities while remaining adaptable to changing situations?
- In what areas might my boundaries be overly rigid?

Like riverbanks, boundaries must balance strength and flexibility. If they are too rigid or weak, adjustments are necessary to maintain effective leadership.

Navigating the currents: Ensuring clarity in communication

- Have I clearly communicated my boundaries, and does the school community understand them?
- Are there implicit or unspoken boundaries that are causing confusion or misalignment?

Transparent communication ensures boundaries are understood and prevents misalignment within the school.

Monitoring erosion: Preventing the gradual weakening of boundaries

- Am I allowing boundaries to erode by becoming too involved in areas others should manage?
- How can I reinforce my boundaries to keep my leadership focused and effective?

Over time, boundaries can erode, much like riverbanks can wear down by constant flow. Principals must monitor where their boundaries might weaken, leading to overinvolvement or burnout.

Maintaining the flow: Balancing influence and autonomy

- How am I balancing my leadership's influence with fostering autonomy in others?
- Are there areas where my leadership might be overstepping?

Balancing leadership influence with others' independence ensures a supportive, not restrictive, leadership style.

> Reflecting on boundaries is like evaluating a river's flow; it's an ongoing process requiring adaptation and clarity. Well-defined boundaries guide a principal's leadership with purpose, enabling them to steer their school with integrity and intention.

Summary

The boundaries a principal establishes and maintains are like riverbanks in that they give shape to their leadership. They direct a principal's influence, define their responsibilities, and ensure that their leadership is channelled purposefully and productively. Without these boundaries, leadership can become a chaotic torrent, eroding the foundation of the school community it aims to build.

A rigid riverbank can stifle the river's flow, just as inflexible boundaries can stifle creativity and collaboration within a school. Conversely, weak boundaries can lead to overinvolvement, burnout, and a blurring of roles that diminishes leadership effectiveness.

Boundary leadership is not just about the boundaries principals set for themselves; it's equally about respecting the boundaries of others. Boundary leadership requires a deep sensitivity to the personal and professional boundaries of the school community—teachers, staff, students, and parents alike. Leadership boundaries allow principals to lead with clarity, purpose, and resilience. Like the banks of a river, they channel the flow of leadership toward meaningful goals, preventing the "flooding" of energy into areas where it is less effective. When maintained with care, they ensure that a principal's leadership flows purposefully, sustainably, and with the most significant possible impact on the school community.

Chapter 32

Seeing clearly, deciding fairly: Principals as judicious leaders

Leadership is full of moments that test a principal's discernment. Standing at the helm of a school is much like presiding over a courtroom—not in the sense of delivering rulings from a place of detached authority, but in the quiet, weighty responsibility of making decisions that shape lives. Every choice, from discipline policies to staffing decisions, carries consequences that ripple through the community. And like a judge, a principal must balance competing interests, uphold ethical standards, and ensure that fairness and justice remain at the heart of every action.

But unlike a judge in a courtroom where laws and precedents dictate decisions, a principal navigates a more complex and fluid reality. Policies provide guidance, but they rarely offer a definitive answer to the nuanced human challenges of a school. Each case that lands on a principal's desk—whether it's a conflict between teachers, a struggling student, or a challenging parental concern—requires a careful weighing of facts, perspectives, and emotions. It is in these moments that a principal's true leadership emerges, not from a place of rigid authority, but from a deep commitment to fairness, integrity, and the well-being of the entire school community.

A principal's decisions, like a judge's rulings, set precedents. Every choice signals to staff, students, and families what matters most in the school's culture. When a principal consistently approaches problems with fairness, thoughtfulness, and clarity, the school community begins to trust in the process. Integrity becomes more than just an abstract value—it becomes a lived experience, woven into the fabric of daily interactions.

Consider a disciplinary case involving a student. A punitive response might seem like the simplest solution—enforcing the rules, demonstrating consistency—but what does it teach? What message does it send about how the school sees children who make mistakes? A principal who leads with discernment doesn't just enforce consequences; they seek to understand the full context of a student's actions, listen to different perspectives, and consider the long-term impact of their decision. Will this choice foster growth and accountability, or will it reinforce cycles of disengagement and exclusion? The answer is rarely simple. It requires patience, inquiry, and the courage to hold space for complexity.

An essential part of this process is actively listening to and incorporating diverse perspectives. This inclusivity enhances the decision-making process and fosters a sense of trust within the school community, ensuring that decisions reflect collective wisdom. The value of this open-mindedness in making the school community feel valued and a part of the decision-making process cannot be overstated.

Every choice a principal makes reinforces the values of the school. Decisions should not be made in isolation, nor should they be reactive. Instead, they should be guided by an unwavering commitment to fairness, reflection, and the well-being of both individuals and the larger community. This is not easy work. It requires emotional intelligence, humility, and a willingness to hold discomfort. But when a principal leads with integrity, when they listen with intention, when they embrace the complexity of their role with both wisdom and heart, they don't just make decisions—they build trust. And trust is what allows a school to thrive.

What this looks like

The gavel of fairness
Like a diligent judge who listens attentively to all arguments before ruling, the principal should ensure that all perspectives are carefully considered and respected before making decisions. The principal must approach conflicts and issues with transparency and fairness, consistently communicating

decisions that align with their integrity. This approach fosters trust and harmony within the school community, promoting a more equitable learning environment.

Refining judicious skills
Making informed and wise decisions requires regular practice and continual improvement. Principals must engage in ongoing learning, self-assessment, and adaptation to guarantee that their decisions consistently embody wisdom, fairness, and ethical principles. This skill cannot be taken for granted; it must be developed and maintained through persistent effort and a dedication to personal development.

The role of reflective practice
Reflective practice is an essential part of improving informed decision-making skills. It is crucial for principals, as engaging in regular reflection allows them to thoroughly evaluate the impact of their decisions and adjust their strategies as necessary. This deliberate process encourages school leaders to pinpoint areas for improvement, draw valuable lessons from past experiences, and effectively apply this knowledge to tackle future challenges.

Collaborative deliberations
Improving one's decision-making skills involves collaborating closely with colleagues and seeking guidance from mentors. Principals can benefit from different perspectives and constructive feedback on their decision-making approaches by actively engaging in a supportive professional community. Exposure to various methods for handling similar challenges is essential for principals to enhance their decision-making abilities.

> Making thoughtful decisions is not a fixed skill; it improves with practice. As principals enhance this skill, their ability to make fair and just decisions will improve, ensuring an equitable decision-making process.

Recognizing blind spots

Overreliance on protocol
Like judges relying heavily on legal precedents, school principals may depend too much on established policies. Strict adherence to established policies can hinder creativity and adaptability. While protocols provide structure, inflexible application may overlook the nuances of individual cases, preventing tailored solutions to specific challenges. This rigidity can erode the school culture and reduce the principal's responsiveness to the community's unique needs.

Misinterpretation of silence
Silence is not always agreement. Teachers, students, or parents who fail to provide feedback may feel uncertain, indifferent, or dissatisfied rather than supportive. Principals must actively seek input and encourage open communication to understand their community's thoughts and emotions, preventing misunderstandings and fostering trust.

Inadequate deliberation
Judges take the time they need to deliberate. But principals, facing external pressures and the other demands of the job, might rush their decisions. Hasty decisions can lead to mistakes or oversights that impact the school's operations and community trust. It's important to remember that the consequences of rushing can be significant and potentially lead to decisions that are not in the school community's best interest.

Compromised transparency
Transparency is crucial for maintaining trust. Even with good intentions, withholding information can foster suspicion among staff, students, and parents. Clear and open communication about decision-making processes strengthens perceptions of the principal's integrity and builds community support.

Underestimation of external influences

Judges must consider the impact of public opinion and the media on their cases, and principals similarly need to recognize external influences, such as community politics, social media, and district policies. Accounting for these factors is essential to avoid missteps. By staying attuned to the broader context, principals can make more informed and effective decisions.

Principals, like judges, must balance the scales of fairness, wisdom, and ethical integrity within their schools. Like judges, they evaluate evidence, consider diverse perspectives, and make decisions that impact the entire community.

Reflective prompts

Weighing the evidence: Balanced judgment
- Am I weighing all the evidence impartially, or is my judgment swayed by certain voices?
- Am I ensuring that personal biases do not affect my decision-making?

Principals, like judges, must ensure every voice is heard and impartially weigh all evidence to make fair and balanced decisions.

Gathering testimony: Understanding context
- Have I gathered all relevant testimony and evidence before reaching a verdict?
- Am I considering the context and background information of everyone involved?

Understanding the broader context helps principals make well-informed and effective decisions, ensuring fairness for all parties.

Considering the verdict: Impact on the school community
- What will be the short-term and long-term consequences of my verdict on the school community?
- How will this decision shape the culture and climate of the school?

Decisions must consider their ripple effects, influencing the well-being of students, staff, and the wider school environment.

Upholding the law: Alignment with mission and values
- Does this verdict align with the school's mission and uphold our core values?
- Am I reflecting the ethical standards and principles of our community?

A principal's decision should reflect the school's mission, values, and district policy.

Shaping precedent: Cultivating a legacy of ethical leadership
- What precedent am I setting with this decision?
- How can my current actions serve as a model for future principals and leaders?

Navigating decision-making with balance and ethical integrity allows principals to lead thoughtfully and ensure their choices foster trust, equity, and positive outcomes for the entire school community.

> Principals should engage in thorough and thoughtful decision-making processes, similar to how a judge carefully evaluates evidence before ruling. This involves weighing the pros and cons, considering the impact on the school community, and ensuring that decisions align with the principal's ethical framework and mission.

Summary

Like judges, principals are entrusted with making decisions that may significantly impact their communities. This demands careful and reflective evaluation of various factors, including policies, student needs, staff dynamics, and community expectations. An essential aspect of effective leadership is actively listening to and incorporating diverse perspectives. Principals should value the viewpoints of teachers, students, parents, and the community, fostering a sense of trust and confidence in the school's leadership.

Chapter 33

Beyond the fog: Navigating liminal spaces

Leadership can feel like walking through a fog-filled forest. The forest represents a liminal space—an uncertain, transitional period of change—between the moment a problem appears and the response it demands. For principals, it can be challenging to guide a school through liminal spaces, when the "fog" limits visibility, the path forward is unclear, and familiar landmarks are hidden from view. These are periods where what was is no longer, and what will be has yet to fully emerge. But these periods are also rich with opportunities for growth and transformation.

For school leaders, liminal spaces may appear during times of organizational change, when initiatives take root, or when conflicts challenge the community's equilibrium. These moments are not voids but opportunities to reimagine, realign, and rebuild. They invite leaders to step into the discomfort of ambiguity with curiosity and humility, embracing the questions that arise rather than rushing to find answers.

In a fog-filled forest, it's impossible to see the whole journey at once. Similarly, principals leading in a liminal space won't always have immediate clarity about the future. Rather than seeking instant answers, they cultivate trust in the process, allowing flexibility to emerge as they adapt to changing circumstances. This mindset encourages patience and an openness to discovering solutions as they go rather than forcing premature conclusions.

Victor Frankl's insight in *Man's Search for Meaning* resonates deeply in thinking about leadership in the liminal space: "Between stimulus and response, there is a space. In that space, we have the power to choose our response." As a principal emerges from the fog-filled forest, having navigated its twists and shadows, they realize that the journey through uncertainty was never about finding a perfectly clear path.

Navigating transitional phases requires patience, curiosity, and strategic thinking. It's essential to recognize that the situation may not resolve as quickly as desired and that the way forward may not be immediately apparent. Leadership, like life, is filled with moments where clarity comes only in tiny glimpses—enough to take the next step. But with each step taken, confidence and capacity grow.

Principals who learn to trust the process, to embrace the fog, know that the journey is not about having all the answers but about asking the right questions, staying curious, and continually reflecting on the path they've travelled. The forest will always be there, presenting new challenges and uncertainties, but they understand that these are opportunities for growth, not barriers. The fog no longer paralyzes—it sharpens focus. An effective principal learns not only to master the terrain, but to walk through it with intention and courage.

What this looks like

Stepping into the fog
In a fog-filled forest, each step must be taken carefully, with a focus on what's immediately visible. Similarly, a principal navigating liminal spaces must break down complex changes into manageable steps, ensuring each action feels achievable and intentional. Instead of overwhelming staff with the entire scope of an initiative, they focus on small, visible steps, guiding the community forward without rushing. Being willing to move forward, even when the destination is unclear, is essential for effective leadership.

Guiding through the forest with vision and flexibility
The principal's vision is like a guiding light for the school community, helping it confront and overcome various challenges. This vision is not rigid but adaptable, like a hiker adjusting their path while navigating a dense forest. Adaptability is evident in strategic planning sessions, where diverse input is

genuinely valued, and in the flexibility of policies and practices that adjust to the evolving needs of the school community.

Cultivating reflection and shared learning

Leading in liminal spaces requires leaving room for reflection and shared learning. Just as hikers pause to assess their surroundings, a principal encourages the school community to reflect on what's working, what isn't, and what can be improved. Collaborative reflection allows staff to feel ownership of the process and strengthens their connection to the change.

> School leaders should understand that moving through liminal spaces requires patience, empathy, and trust-building. By embodying courage, strategic thinking, and adaptability, principals help their school community navigate uncertainty with confidence. Their thoughtful actions transform the foggy path of change into a meaningful journey toward growth and a brighter future.

Recognizing blind spots

The illusion of visibility

It's easy for principals to assume that they fully understand the school's needs and challenges during times of change. However, decisions made with limited visibility may not address the deeper complexities at play. Principals must actively seek broader perspectives and listen deeply to truly understand the community's needs. This means regularly stepping back, asking questions, and being open to the insights of others.

The echoes of past paths

Relying on familiar strategies offers comfort but can also keep school leaders stuck. What worked in the past may not be what's needed in today's climate of uncertainty. Principals often lean on proven methods, assuming they will continue to be effective. Leaders must recognize when traditional strategies no longer serve their school community's best interests and be willing to explore new directions, even if uncertain of the outcome.

The mirage of quick fixes

When leaders feel pressured to address uncertainty quickly, they may feel tempted to implement fast fixes that promise immediate results. However, these speedy solutions may only provide temporary relief without addressing the root causes. Principals should resist the pull of immediate results and instead embrace a slower, more deliberate approach. Sustainable progress requires patience, perseverance, and a willingness to delve into the situation's complexities.

The shadows of isolation

School leaders may think they have to deal with everything alone, which can stop them from getting helpful advice and support from teachers, students, parents, and the wider community. Like a complex ecosystem in a forest, the school community is full of wisdom and strength. Working together to solve problems and sharing leadership can help a principal find the best way forward more effectively than trying to do it alone.

The distortion of scale

Fog can distort the perceived scale of obstacles, making challenges seem more daunting than they are. This distortion can lead to hesitation or inaction, stalling the school's progress. Principals should develop the ability to assess accurately the actual size and significance of obstacles while balancing realism and optimism.

Relying too heavily on reflection without action

Working in liminal spaces often involves a reflective phase, during which the school community evaluates past practices and considers new approaches. Principals who remain in "reflection mode" may unintentionally delay progress, leaving staff feeling as if they're stuck in the fog rather than moving forward.

By acknowledging the limitations of visibility, the influence of past experiences, the allure of quick fixes, the impact of isolation, and the distortion of perspective, principals can lead with greater insight and adaptability, empowering them to guide their school community through challenges with clarity and purpose.

Reflective prompts

Illuminating the path: Vision and values in the mist
- How do I stay true to our school's vision as I navigate the fog of daily challenges?
- In unexpected situations, do my responses reflect my core values?

Reflecting on these questions helps principals ensure their immediate actions align with long-term goals and ethical commitments.

Listening to the whispers of the woods: Community voices
- What steps am I taking to hear the faint voices in the forest?
- In recent decisions, how have I addressed the needs of our school community's more secluded areas?

Principals should actively seek and consider feedback from all sectors of the school community, especially from those less heard.

Adapting to the terrain: Flexibility in uncharted areas
- How have I adjusted my compass when the terrain shifts unexpectedly?
- What lessons have I learned from navigating the toughest challenges?

Navigating uncharted territories encourages a mindset of continuous learning and agility in leadership practices.

Reaching the forest's edge: Visioning beyond current boundaries
- As I approach the forest's edge, what do I hope to find on the other side?
- What preparations are necessary to ensure our community is ready to step out of the forest and into new landscapes?

Navigating uncertainty encourages principals to think beyond the current context's immediate confines and envision future possibilities.

> By reflecting regularly on vision, values, and community needs, principals navigate the fog of uncertainty with intentionality and resilience. This practice ensures thoughtful, aligned actions that balance immediate demands with long-term aspirations, creating a school environment primed for growth and transformation.

Summary

Navigating liminal spaces in school leadership is similar to moving through a fog-filled forest. Principals must guide their communities through uncertainty with patience, adaptability, and vision. These transitional moments can feel disorienting and challenging, but they are also rich with opportunities for meaningful change, discovery, and growth.

Hikers rely on their senses and instincts when familiar markers are obscured; principals must become more attuned to the needs and aspirations of their school community. This involves slowing down, paying closer attention to subtle signals from students, staff, and parents, and being open to innovative problem-solving approaches.

Embracing uncertainty and ambiguity requires courage, adaptability, and a collaborative spirit. Ultimately, the ability to lead through liminal spaces enables the school to emerge stronger from transitional moments and cultivates a community ready to embrace future challenges with confidence and unity.

Chapter 34

Riding the rapids: Successfully leading change

Leading change as a principal is like navigating the rapids of a rushing river. The water flows fiercely, presenting unexpected obstacles and swiftly changing currents. In this chaotic environment, the principal steers purposefully, understanding the river's rhythms and reading the turbulent waters ahead to chart a strategic path forward. Leading change demands precision, resilience, and the courage to adapt quickly to new challenges while keeping the crew focused and working toward the collective goal.

Understanding the people who are being led through a process of change is crucial because it impacts their lives. John Kotter, a professor at the Harvard Business School, outlined a strategic process for managing change in his influential work, *Leading Change*.

Successfully guiding people through change requires understanding their perspectives, concerns, and aspirations. Change is not just an organizational shift—it impacts the daily lives, emotions, and professional identities of those involved. Effective leadership in change management requires both strategy and empathy, ensuring that transitions are not imposed but embraced.

The process begins with creating a sense of urgency, helping people understand why the change is necessary and how it aligns with their shared values. Leading through change is about fostering commitment, not about forcing compliance. When leaders engage people in the process, address concerns with transparency, and celebrate progress, change becomes an opportunity for growth rather than a source of resistance. By modelling adaptability, reinforcing shared goals, and embedding new practices into the school's culture, principals can ensure that change is not just implemented but sustained.

A skilled river guide reads the river's currents, anticipating changes and making real-time adjustments to keep the raft on course. Similarly, a principal must be adept at reading the "currents" of the school, sensing where resistance might arise and navigating it with empathy and strategy. Resistance to change is natural, and a principal's ability to manage it effectively can make the difference between progress and getting stuck in the rapids. Managing resistance requires a balance of flexibility and firmness, staying true to the vision while being responsive to the community's needs and concerns. It also requires an understanding of the importance of identifying key points along the route. For a river guide, those are navigable rapids, calm stretches, and landmarks that signal progress. For a principal, they are actionable goals that break up the vision into manageable milestones. These goals provide a sense of achievement, keep the momentum alive, and ensure that progress is measured and celebrated throughout the change process.

Change leadership is about the journey itself more than reaching a destination. It's about learning to "read the river," adjusting to changing conditions, and celebrating successes along the way. By fostering a culture of trust, collaboration, and resilience, principals who effectively lead through change ensure that the school community not only survives the journey but thrives, emerging stronger and more united on the other side.

What this looks like

Setting a clear course

A river guide begins any journey by mapping a clear course, and a principal leading change does the same by creating a compelling vision that inspires the school community. This vision acts as a guiding compass, providing clarity about the destination and how to get there. A principal communicates this vision clearly and consistently, ensuring that staff, students, and parents understand the reasons behind the change and the expected outcomes.

CHAPTER 34

Building buy-in and trust

Just as a river guide needs a reliable crew to navigate the waters, a principal leading change must cultivate trust and buy-in from the school community. This means involving stakeholders early and often, listening to concerns, and valuing the input of teachers, students, and parents. A principal who acts like a river guide knows that change is a team effort, and they work to create a sense of ownership and shared responsibility.

Adjusting along the way

A river guide makes real-time adjustments based on the changing conditions. Similarly, a principal leading change must be flexible and adaptable, using data and feedback to monitor progress and make course corrections when necessary. This means being willing to shift strategies, refine goals, or adjust timelines in response to what's happening in the school community.

Providing stability in turbulent waters

A river guide remains calm and composed, even when the waters get choppy. A principal leading change must also stay steady and focused, especially during times of resistance or unexpected setbacks. This means maintaining a clear sense of direction while being empathetic to the concerns of staff, students, and parents. By modelling composure, a principal reassures the school community that they are capable of navigating the difficulties together.

> To effectively lead change in a school, a principal sets a clear course, builds trust with their crew, empowers staff to take risks, monitors progress, and celebrates successes—all while remaining calm and composed in the face of challenges.

OPERATIONAL LEADERSHIP

Recognizing blind spots

Underestimating complexity
Change in a school environment often affects deep-rooted habits, systems, and cultural dynamics that are not easily altered. When change doesn't unfold as quickly or as smoothly as anticipated, overlooking these complexities can lead to frustration and setbacks. Principals should recognize that change is rarely a linear process; it requires time, patience, and attention to the nuances that make each school unique.

Rushing the process
While enthusiasm and urgency are valuable traits, moving too fast can overwhelm staff, create resistance, and hinder the sustainability of change efforts. To navigate this challenge, principals need to pace themselves and the school community, focusing on a few high-impact changes and providing ample time for reflection and adjustment along the way. Change is best navigated in stages, allowing the community to develop confidence before tackling the next set of rapids.

Ignoring resistance
A principal leading change may fall into the blind spot of ignoring resistance within the school community, hoping that opposition will fade over time. However, resistance is often a sign of deeper concerns that need to be addressed. Ignoring it can increase frustration, disengagement, and even sabotage change efforts.

Complacency after early success
Sustainable change requires ongoing attention, maintenance, and adaptation. Early successes can lose momentum without continued focus, and the change effort can stall. For example, if a principal launches a successful literacy program and then shifts focus to other priorities, they might overlook the need for continued professional development, resources, and follow-up support. To address this challenge, principals should celebrate successes while keeping a watchful eye on the change effort, ensuring that momentum

is maintained and any necessary adjustments are made over time. Leading through change is a marathon, not a sprint, and sustained vigilance is crucial.

Oversteering the process

A principal leading change may fall into oversteering—micromanaging the process instead of empowering staff to take ownership. This can lead to a lack of autonomy, disengagement, and a sense that the change is being imposed rather than collaboratively developed. To avoid this blind spot, principals should trust their staff, provide clear guidance, and then step back, allowing teachers to navigate the specifics in a way that suits their unique contexts. Empowering staff to lead within the change framework is essential for building a shared leadership and sustainability culture.

> Principals who embrace the mindset of a river guide understand that leading change is a dynamic journey requiring flexibility, trust, and continual learning. With their eyes fixed on the horizon of a brighter future, principals guide their schools toward meaningful transformation, one current at a time.

Reflective prompts

Charting the course: Vision and planning

- Is my vision clear and compelling, serving as a beacon for the school community?
- Have I broken the journey into actionable steps that everyone can follow?

A principal must have a clear vision that serves as a guiding star for the school community.

Steering the raft: Balancing leadership with empathy

- How effectively am I balancing strategic leadership with empathy and support?

- How well am I adapting my approach to respond to any emerging challenges?

Reflecting on adaptability ensures that the principal can adjust their leadership approach as new challenges arise.

Reading the river: Addressing resistance
- Am I actively listening to concerns from staff, students, or parents and exploring the reasons behind resistance?
- Have I used resistance as an opportunity to uncover valid concerns or address misunderstandings?

Resistance signals significant undercurrents that require attention. Principals who reflect on their response to opposition can transform challenges into opportunities for dialogue and growth.

Adjusting the course: Am I remaining flexible?
- Do I regularly collect and analyze data to monitor the impact of changes?
- Am I open to revising plans based on feedback and evidence from staff and students?

Reflecting on their own willingness to change course when necessary helps principals remain responsive and data-driven, ensuring that the change efforts are effective and relevant.

> Leading change is an ongoing journey that requires thoughtful planning, adaptability, and a willingness to listen and adjust. By regularly engaging in reflective questioning, principals ensure that their leadership remains intentional and responsive. Like a skilled river guide, they keep their team on course, confidently navigating challenges and uniting the school community around shared goals.

CHAPTER 34

Summary

Change is inherently uncertain. Leading through change requires a deep understanding of the school's culture, the courage to challenge the status quo, and the resilience to face setbacks without losing sight of the destination. A principal who leads change is more than a manager of tasks; they are a navigator, a motivator, a listener, and an empowerer. They understand that change is not a solitary endeavour but a collective journey where every school community member plays a vital role. Through it all, a principal's ability to communicate a compelling vision, build trust, empower staff, and celebrate progress is critical.

Yet, even with the best-laid plans, leading change is rarely a linear path. Moments of turbulence, resistance, and unexpected challenges will test any leader's resolve. Flexibility is not a sign of weakness; it is a recognition that the conditions are constantly shifting, and a leader's ability to adapt ensures the journey's success.

By leading with curiosity, clarity, and compassion, principals transform not only a school's structures and practices but also the mindset and beliefs of the entire community. This is the true power of effective leadership: inspiring a collective movement toward a better, more inclusive, and more dynamic future.

PART 6

Equity-Centred Leadership

Chapter 35

Mirror, mirror: Embracing ontological humility

Imagine a principal stepping into their office early in the morning as the school comes alive. Instead of a regular mirror on the wall, there is a "mirror of reality." This mirror doesn't merely reflect the principal's image; it exposes their beliefs, biases shaped by personal experiences, and the varied perspectives they encounter daily on the job. Every decision the principal makes and every interaction they have with students, teachers, and parents reflects what this mirror shows.

Ontological humility is the practice of acknowledging that everyone views the world through the lens of their own beliefs, experiences, and assumptions, and that other views are valid. For principals, practising ontological humility begins by recognizing that their leadership position doesn't give them a monopoly on wisdom, and that there are many ways to interpret and understand the same situation. It requires a deep awareness that their own experiences shape their perceptions, which limit their ability to fully understand the diverse realities within the school community. This awareness allows for a more diverse and inclusive approach to leadership.

Research in educational leadership consistently emphasizes the importance of self-awareness and emotional intelligence in establishing practical, compassionate, and responsive school environments. Principals may be tempted to lead from a place of certainty, but authentic leadership comes from a willingness to question their assumptions and listen more deeply.

For example, when a principal receives a complaint from a teacher about a colleague's unfair treatment, their initial reaction may be shaped by their personal experiences or past interactions with those involved. Practising ontological humility means resisting the urge to rely solely on those past impressions and instead seeking multiple perspectives before forming a judgment. It means asking, "What might I be missing?" rather than assuming they already know the full picture.

Developing ontological humility has many benefits. It helps principals understand their personal experiences, beliefs, and biases shape their world view. It positively impacts decision-making, interactions with staff and students, and the overall approach to school management and leadership. In an environment that values ontological humility, the principal makes decisions collaboratively, considering diverse perspectives. For example, when a leader openly says, "I may not fully understand your experience. Help me see it from your perspective," they validate others' viewpoints and build stronger connections. Over time, this openness fosters psychological safety, encouraging more honest conversations and collaborative problem-solving.

By practising ontological humility, principals demonstrate to the school community that authentic leadership is an evolving journey. They let the mirror of ontological humility shape their path, guiding them toward being more compassionate, effective, and responsive.

What this looks like

The mirror of vulnerability

Leading with ontological humility means being open about one's own mistakes and areas for growth. A principal who embodies this trait does not shy away from admitting when they are wrong or that a decision didn't have the desired impact. Instead, they see these moments as opportunities to model vulnerability and a growth mindset for the entire school. By admitting mistakes, they demonstrate that vulnerability is a strength and everyone can learn and grow, regardless of their role.

The mirror of responsive leadership

Responsive leadership adapts to the evolving needs of the school community. A principal practising ontological humility is open to changing their leadership strategies based on new information or feedback. The principal's adaptability is evident in how they implement and adjust policies, showcasing a flexible approach. They revisit decisions, communicate changes, and explain the reasons behind shifts in direction, all while prioritizing the school community's best interests.

The mirror of equity and fairness

A principal who leads with ontological humility consistently reviews policies and practices to ensure fairness and equity for all students, staff, and community members. This involves examining disciplinary actions, resource allocation, and program accessibility to align all decisions with the principles of fairness and equity. The principal's dedication to addressing disparities and fostering a culture of equity within the school is demonstrated through their actions, not just their words.

The mirror of accountability

School principals should hold themselves and their schools to high standards of integrity and performance. This means being accountable to the community for the school's outcomes and leadership shortcomings. A principal's willingness to take personal responsibility for failures and celebrate collective successes demonstrates ontological humility.

> Ultimately, ontological humility is about leading with a mindset of inquiry, continually learning about the world and its people. It's about holding space for multiple truths, leading to a more prosperous, more inclusive leadership practice that strengthens a principal's leadership.

Recognizing blind spots

The edges of the mirror: Assuming complete knowledge

The frame of a mirror represents the boundaries that school principals may face in fully understanding their school community. Principals who rely heavily on their knowledge and experiences may overlook important insights and nuances. Assuming complete knowledge can overshadow the insights of teachers, students, and parents. By acknowledging the limitations of their viewpoint, principals can actively seek and appreciate the perspectives of others, thus promoting a more comprehensive and inclusive understanding of the school environment.

Reflections coloured by bias

The mirror of leadership can highlight certain biases more prominently, revealing the prejudices that shape a principal's perceptions. These conscious or unconscious biases can significantly affect how principals view situations and make decisions. For example, a principal might show favouritism toward specific teachers or student groups, resulting in unfairness and inequity within the school. Principals need to recognize these biases to make more objective decisions.

Resisting the mirror's truth

The mirror of ontological humility can sometimes reflect aspects that are uncomfortable to acknowledge. Avoiding these truths can hinder growth as a leader and resisting the need to be open to change. To overcome this blind spot, principals must embrace feedback from all school community members while withholding judgment or bias.

Missing the value hidden in cracks

Mirrors sometimes crack; in this metaphor, a crack in the mirror can symbolize a failure or setback. These cracks can provide valuable lessons if viewed as opportunities for learning and growth. Embracing setbacks as opportunities for learning can lead to greater resilience and a more informed approach to leadership. By reflecting on what went wrong and why, principals can develop more effective strategies and techniques for the future. It is important to remember that leading with ontological humility requires leaders to openly and honestly address their shortcomings to improve their leadership capacity.

CHAPTER 35

Looking through the ontological mirror is invaluable for school principals committed to effective and inclusive leadership. It enables them to reflect on their practices, engage with their school community, and pursue continual learning.

Reflective prompts

The mirror of self-perception

- How might my values and experiences limit my understanding of others' perspectives?
- In what ways have I changed my views based on interactions with others in the school community?

Reflecting on self-perception helps principals recognize biases and identify opportunities to broaden their understanding.

The mirror of inclusivity

- Have I consulted a diverse range of voices before making significant decisions?
- What steps have I taken to ensure underrepresented groups in my school feel heard and empowered?

Reflecting on these questions is essential for fostering an inclusive school culture where every member feels valued.

The mirror of adaptability

- How do I handle situations when evidence or feedback contradicts my assumptions or beliefs?
- What practices have I changed this year based on feedback from the school community?

Adapting views and perspectives in light of new information is essential for school leaders.

The mirror of impact
- Which of my actions have positively or negatively affected the school culture this year?
- How do I know if my leadership benefits all students and staff?

Understanding the true impact of the actions taken by a principal is essential in calibrating their approach to school leadership.

> By embracing ontological humility, principals create a leadership style grounded in self-awareness, adaptability, and inclusivity. Regularly reflecting on their biases, the diversity of perspectives they consult, and the tangible impact of their actions allows them to foster a school culture rooted in trust and shared growth.

Summary

By embracing the metaphorical mirror of ontological humility, principals can refine their leadership to align more closely with the diverse needs and aspirations of their school communities. Recognizing that their perspective is just one part of a larger narrative helps leaders see their role clearly and value the varied stories that shape their schools. Ontological humility calls on principals to acknowledge limitations, challenge assumptions, and welcome insights from others, fostering a leadership style grounded in learning and openness.

This mindset reshapes how principals approach feedback, transforming criticism from a perceived threat to a vital learning opportunity. Feedback becomes a lens through which leaders can understand how others experience their leadership. By modelling receptiveness to feedback, principals promote a culture of growth and learning across the school.

Leading with ontological humility ensures that staff, students, and parents feel heard, respected, and empowered to share their insights. By fostering an environment of trust, empathy, and shared leadership, principals build a resilient school culture in which every voice contributes to collective success.

Chapter 36

Navigating the undercurrents: Subversive leadership

Imagine a vast ocean. It is calm on the surface, yet hidden beneath the tranquil surface are powerful undercurrents that influence everything in their path. This metaphor captures the essence of subversive leadership. Much like the deep, unseen ocean undercurrents, subversive leadership operates below the surface, shaping and influencing the environment in ways that are not always immediately visible.

Fei Wang, in "Subversive Leadership and Power Tactics," published in the *Journal of Education Administration*, emphasizes that effective school leaders must navigate institutional constraints while resisting policies and practices that marginalize, using thoughtful disruption to create more equitable and inclusive learning environments. Subversive leadership for principals involves using influence and strategic thinking to bend, but not break, the rules to serve the greater good. In a system often bound by rigid policies and traditional practices, subversive school leaders recognize that leading sometimes requires going beyond what is explicitly allowed. Principals who adopt this approach understand that while rules and policies are essential, they must serve the greater good. They know the official rules don't always account for the complex realities of their school communities and that to ensure every student has a fair chance to succeed, they may need to navigate these boundaries with creativity and courage.

For example, a zero-tolerance policy might unintentionally disadvantage marginalized students. Instead of strict enforcement, a subversive leader might create support programs that address behaviour concerns more equitably, ensuring every student has the opportunity to succeed.

Much like undercurrents, subversive leaders do not always announce their intentions or seek immediate recognition. Instead, they work below the waves of school culture, quietly moving toward meaningful change. In schools, subversive leadership can take the form of advocating for more inclusive practices, even when district policy seems inflexible. It might mean supporting a teacher in trying a bold, new approach to curriculum delivery that doesn't align with traditional expectations. These leaders create space for innovation and experimentation, knowing that real growth often begins with subtle ripples. They ask the quiet, hard questions: Whose voices aren't being heard here? Who is being left behind? What hidden assumptions are shaping this decision?

Subversive leadership is not without risks. Principals may encounter resistance from those invested in maintaining the status quo or colleagues who view their actions as too radical. Managing these risks requires careful planning and, sometimes, a willingness to stand alone.

What this looks like

Shaping change beneath the surface

Like the undercurrents of the ocean, subversive leadership operates beneath the visible policies of the school. School leaders challenge the status quo through strategic and quiet influence. Principals who practise subversive leadership recognize that to create lasting change, they must work within these unseen layers, subtly shifting the direction of their school toward an equitable and inclusive school culture.

The power of subtle influence

A principal's quiet, subversive leadership might appear small or incremental, much like the gentle push of an undercurrent. However, these subtle influences accumulate over time, creating significant shifts in the school environment. A subversive principal might quietly adjust the application of a school-wide policy to better serve marginalized students, ensuring they have the resources and support needed to thrive. This might involve reinterpreting disciplinary policies to focus on restorative practices rather than punitive measures, or subtly advocating for more inclusive curricula that reflect the diverse backgrounds of the student body. The entire community may not always see these actions, but they deeply feel their impact as the culture gradually shifts toward inclusivity and compassion.

Building trust and collaboration

Subversive leadership, like an undercurrent, is not immediately visible but deeply felt. A sincere dedication to listening and understanding the needs of all stakeholders characterizes this type of leadership, ensuring that changes are developed collaboratively rather than imposed from above. It might manifest as increased student engagement as the school community begins to reflect the values of equity and justice that the principal subtly advocates for. Over time, these visible changes reinforce the underlying currents of subversive leadership, making the school a place where every community member feels valued and supported.

> Subversive leadership doesn't make waves; it creates currents. Through persistent, quiet efforts, subversive principals reshape their schools, aligning them with the principles of equity, justice, and compassion. While their actions may be understated, their long-term impact is deeply felt across the school community.

Recognizing blind spots

The depth deception: Forgetting to balance subtlety with direct action

A principal may believe their subtle nudges are enough to guide the school culture toward desired outcomes. However, without clear indicators of success, it can be challenging to measure the effectiveness of this approach. Principals must regularly bring these underlying issues to the surface by making implicit issues explicit through feedback and open dialogue to assess their impact accurately. Relying solely on subtle tactics can lead to delays or inadequate responses to critical challenges.

Navigational hazards: Losing sight of the shore
Principals can lose sight of their strategic vision like captains distracted by immediate sea conditions. Regularly evaluating alignment with the school's mission and adapting to broader trends—such as societal changes or policy shifts—keeps efforts relevant and impactful. Maintaining focus on the larger picture ensures that day-to-day actions contribute to long-term success.

Turbulence: Navigating unintended consequences
Subversive leadership can have unintended consequences, and unexpected outcomes can arise from well-meaning actions. For example, introducing a new policy without fully considering its implementation could overwhelm staff or create unforeseen challenges, leading to a breakdown in the consistency of school expectations. To navigate these challenges, principals must remain attentive to the ripple effects of their decisions, regularly gather feedback, and be prepared to make adjustments as needed.

The invisible currents: Overlooking stakeholder perspectives
Although subversive leadership can bring subtle influence and change, principals must actively engage the school community members in decision-making. For example, a principal might introduce an initiative to promote equity. But if the principal does not adequately inform or involve teachers, students, and parents, the initiative may not be as successful as hoped. School community members may feel excluded or confused, leading to resistance or disengagement. To avoid this, principals must actively seek out diverse perspectives, ensuring they consider the voices of all stakeholders.

> Subversive leadership is a nuanced journey that requires reflection, adaptability, and collaboration. By addressing blind spots and navigating risks thoughtfully, principals can harness its power to transform their school communities in meaningful and lasting ways.

Reflective prompts

Questioning the currents: Awareness of influence
- What unspoken messages am I sending through my actions and decisions?
- How might my choices affect less visible or vocal members of the school community?

Subversive leadership often works subtly. Reflecting on these messages helps principals recognize the undercurrents their actions create.

Charting the course: Evaluating impact
- What unintended consequences have arisen, and how can I address them?
- How am I adapting to my school community's changing needs?

Reflecting on unintended consequences helps principals course-correct when necessary, ensuring their leadership remains effective and equitable.

Navigating the undercurrents: Strategic push and measured pull
- How do I balance initiating change with fostering organic development?
- How can I better read and respond to subtle shifts in the school community?

Finding the right balance between initiating change and allowing natural development will help to ensure that reforms are sustainable over time.

Checking the compass: Core values and integrity
- Do my actions reflect the school's core values?
- How do I maintain integrity while navigating complex challenges?

Decisions consistent with core values and integrity build trust and respect, which are crucial for effective subversive leadership.

> Through continual reflection, principals can refine their subversive leadership approach, staying responsive to their community's needs while making significant, lasting improvements. This reflective practice allows principals to harness the quiet power of subversive leadership to create meaningful and enduring change.

Summary

Subversive leadership is like the undercurrents of the ocean—subtle, persistent, and impactful. As principals navigate the complexities of their school communities, they must be aware of the delicate balance between bending the rules to serve the greater good and maintaining the integrity of their leadership. This form of leadership demands a deep understanding of the unseen forces at play, a commitment to equity, and the courage to act in ways that may not always be visible but are nonetheless transformative.

Subversive principals understand the art of influence. They know when to push directly against resistance and when to flow around it like a current circumventing a rock. They don't bulldoze over opposition but strategically build relationships, gently eroding resistance over time. Their leadership is rooted in deep listening, compassion, and a long-term vision for equity and justice. Like the ocean's undercurrents that eventually reshape a coastline, subversive leaders enact change gradually but with profound and lasting impact.

Chapter 37

From roots to canopy: Calmness and stability

Amid the dense forest stands a solitary oak tree. Its roots dig deep into the earth while its branches stretch toward the sky. The oak tree can withstand strong winds and powerful storms, showing stability and strength during chaotic times. Like this oak, a school principal should embody calmness and stability for their community, regardless of the surrounding turbulence.

Calm leadership is a cornerstone of effective school leadership, especially during turbulent times. For principals, embodying calm leadership means remaining steady and grounded, even when the winds of uncertainty and change blow fiercely through the school community.

Like a mighty oak, calm leaders are resilient. They stand firm during challenging moments, providing a sense of safety and predictability when everything else feels chaotic. Whether navigating a crisis, managing unexpected disruptions, or guiding a school through times of uncertainty, these leaders serve as anchors. Their calm demeanour reassures staff, students, and parents alike that, despite the turbulence, there is a reliable force at the helm. This does not mean that leaders conceal their true feelings or aim for flawlessness; instead, it means they develop a leadership style that allows them to handle difficult situations with composure and thoughtful deliberation.

According to a study published in the *Journal of Applied Psychology* by Peter Harms and colleagues, leaders who maintain emotional stability during stressful situations can significantly reduce their team's perceived stress. This finding emphasizes the significant influence of a principal's response to stress in alleviating overall anxiety within the school.

It's essential that the principal standing as the oak in their school community look inward. They must cultivate self-awareness and understand the roots of their emotions and how they influence their leadership. Cultivating self-awareness is not something extra; it's essential for offering stability to others. This will keep a principal grounded in the strongest storms, just like the deep roots of an oak tree.

This kind of leadership offers the stability and resilience necessary for a school to confront challenges boldly, approach change with optimism, and cultivate a culture of growth and progress.

What this looks like

Steady in the storm

When turbulent times hit a school—be it a crisis, a conflict among staff, or external pressures—calm leaders act like the oak tree's trunk, solid and unshaken. They are not immune to the challenges but absorb the impact, offering reassurance through their steady demeanour. In practice, a principal stays composed during difficult conversations, whether with an angry parent or during a heated staff meeting. They acknowledge the tension, but they do not allow themselves to be swept away by it. Instead, they model resilience, offering solutions while keeping emotions in check, helping to de-escalate the situation and restore balance.

Branching out with support

Like an oak tree's expansive branches, calm leaders extend their support widely, creating an environment where staff feel safe to grow and take risks. During periods of significant change, such as implementing a new curriculum or navigating district mandates, a calm principal listens to concerns, validates emotions, and provides reassurance. By staying visible and accessible, they foster a culture of trust and collaboration, encouraging the school community to face challenges together.

Offering shelter and shade

Calm leaders provide a refuge, much like the shade of an oak tree, offering comfort when anxiety runs high. For instance, following a traumatic event, a calm principal avoids rushing to a quick fix, instead setting a steady tone for reflection and healing. Their ability to offer emotional stability allows the community to process challenges with intention, making them a source of strength for students, staff, and families.

> Principals can demonstrate stability and composure within their school communities through daily interactions, decisions, and presence. Their visible calmness sets the tone for a resilient, nurturing, and inclusive school culture.

Recognizing blind spots

Mistaking calm for indifference

A calm leader risks being perceived as indifferent. Staying steady and composed during challenging times can sometimes come across as being emotionally detached or uncaring, especially when staff or students are deeply affected by events. Calm leaders need to balance their steadiness with visible empathy and understanding, showing that while they are calm, they are also deeply engaged and attuned to the emotions around them.

The illusion of permanent calm

Just as an oak tree needs rich soil and sunlight to thrive, leaders must also acknowledge their vulnerabilities and seek support when necessary. Failing to do so can result in burnout, reduced effectiveness, and a growing disconnection from the school community. Understanding the importance of rest and renewal can help leaders maintain their resilience and authenticity. An authentic leader doesn't hide their emotions but nurtures their well-being to continue strengthening others.

Misreading the need for urgency

Sometimes urgency is necessary, and a leader's calm demeanour may be misaligned with the pace that others need. In a fast-moving crisis—such as a sudden safety concern, public relations issue, or rapidly evolving educational mandate—a principal may need to show more visible urgency to reflect the seriousness of the situation. A principal must be aware of when their team or school community requires a sense of immediacy to feel reassured that appropriate action is being taken.

Overlooking subtle signs of distress

Calm leaders may inadvertently overlook subtle signs of distress in their staff or students. While maintaining a calm demeanour, they might not notice when others are struggling beneath the surface. Staff who are highly stressed, overwhelmed, or quietly disengaging might feel uncomfortable voicing their concerns if they perceive the principal as too calm or removed from the emotional pulse of the school. Principals need to balance outward calm with inward attentiveness, ensuring they remain connected to the community's well-being.

> Addressing these potential blind spots can enhance the effectiveness of calm leadership. Like a well-rooted oak tree, principals can provide stability and resilience for their school community while remaining attuned to the nuanced needs and dynamics of the ecosystem they anchor.

Reflective prompts

Roots of serenity: Ground leadership in values

- How do my core values stabilize my leadership during turbulent times?
- How can I deepen these roots to enhance stability during adversity?

Grounding leadership in strong values ensures calmness and reflects inner stability, enabling leaders to guide their schools with serenity through challenging times.

CHAPTER 37

Nurturing the soil: Fostering a fertile environment for growth
- How does my calm demeanour help foster a culture of growth and collaboration?
- How can I ensure that my leadership nurtures the school community's well-being?

A leader's calm approach enriches the school environment, creating fertile ground for innovation and mutual support, allowing the community to thrive like a healthy grove.

Weathering storms: Balancing stability and flexibility
- How do I balance a stable presence while adapting to new challenges?
- What lessons from past challenges can I apply to navigate future storms with resilience?

Calm leaders balance steadiness with adaptability, navigating storms with grace and resilience.

Sustaining the grove: Sharing calm leadership across the team
- How do I model and promote calm leadership among my team?
- How can I encourage others to adopt a consistent, stable approach to challenges?

By fostering calm leadership within their team, principals create a culture of mindfulness and stability that permeates the school, ensuring collective resilience.

> Principals can refine their leadership approach by reflecting on the steadfast oak and balancing calmness with responsiveness. This thoughtful practice ensures stable, inclusive, and nurturing leadership that empowers the school community to grow and thrive together.

Summary

The principal's role resembles an oak tree standing tall in a dense forest, symbolizing steadfastness, resilience, and unwavering support for the school community. The oak tree's sturdy trunk and expansive branches provide shelter and protection, nurturing a thriving space for life. Similarly, a principal's composed leadership creates an environment where educators, students, and staff feel safe, appreciated, and empowered.

Like the oak tree standing firm in the face of powerful winds without snapping, a principal should embody resilience, guiding the school community to confront challenges with grit and embrace change with adaptability. Principals can instill confidence and resilience in their students and teachers through steady guidance and composed leadership.

Calm leadership is a valuable asset for school principals, especially during times of uncertainty and upheaval. It offers support and protection, allowing staff and students to feel safe, think clearly, and thrive despite challenges.

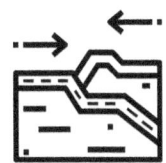

Chapter 38

Tectonic shifts: Challenging the status quo

Far beneath the earth's surface, tectonic plates shift slowly, moving continents and altering the landscape. Although these movements are mostly imperceptible, they gradually create towering mountains, deep valleys, and entirely new terrains. Tectonic shifts mirror the work of principals who lead with the courage to unsettle the right people and challenge the status quo. Like tectonic shifts, their leadership exerts just enough pressure to provoke change without undermining the foundation of the school community.

A principal who leads in this way understands that growth often requires discomfort. They recognize where inertia has taken hold—whether in outdated instructional practices, inequitable policies, or a culture of complacency—and apply the necessary tectonic pressure to shift these entrenched norms. The act of leadership, in this sense, is a deliberate disruption. Without it, the school remains static, unable to adapt to new challenges or seize emerging opportunities. Like the earth's tectonic forces, the principal must create a movement that redefines the terrain.

Research on adaptive leadership, such as the work of Ronald Heifetz and colleagues, emphasizes the importance of creating "productive disequilibrium." This concept aligns with the tectonic metaphor: change must disrupt enough to spark progress but not so much that the system becomes unmanageable. For instance, a principal might challenge teachers entrenched in outdated instructional methods to adopt practices that align with evidence-based instruction. This pressure may feel uncomfortable to those accustomed to the old ways, but it is necessary to elevate teaching and learning to meet the needs of all students.

This approach is not without its risks. Principals who lead in this way must anticipate and manage the potential fallout of their decisions. Some may interpret the shifts as unnecessary upheaval, and those who feel the most pressure may push back, sometimes vehemently, which is why intentionality and clarity are crucial. Leaders must communicate the "why" behind the changes, grounding their actions in the shared values of the school community. They must also create support systems for those who feel disoriented, helping them navigate the shifting terrain with confidence and trust.

Just as tectonic plates take years to reshape landscapes, the impact of these changes may only become fully apparent over time. However, effective school leadership is defined by a commitment to creating meaningful progress, even in the face of discomfort. It is not about avoiding tension or maintaining calm but about embracing the seismic moments that propel a school forward.

What this looks like

Mapping the fault lines
Effective principals first identify where pressure is needed most—what can be considered the "fault lines" in the school's culture or systems. These are often places where outdated practices, inequitable policies, or complacency has taken root. Mapping these areas requires listening, observing, and gathering input from staff, students, and parents. By identifying the fault lines, the principal pinpoints where movement is most needed to create a more vibrant learning environment.

Applying the right pressure
Once the fault lines are identified, the principal must apply deliberate and strategic pressure to provoke movement without destabilizing the entire system. Like tectonic plates that shift incrementally to create significant changes over time, principals introduce challenges in manageable,

phased ways. For instance, a principal might encourage teachers to pilot a student-centred teaching model in select classrooms before rolling it out school-wide. This approach allows the community to adapt gradually, minimizing resistance while building confidence in the new direction.

Managing the friction

As tectonic plates grind against each other during shifts, friction is inevitable—and so is resistance in school leadership. Principals leading transformative change must anticipate resistance and see it as a sign of progress rather than failure. Pushback from some staff or parents is likely when a principal challenges a deeply ingrained grading policy that perpetuates inequities. The principal manages this friction constructively by engaging in transparent conversations, sharing evidence of why the change is necessary, and addressing concerns with empathy. This approach ensures that resistance becomes part of the growth process rather than an obstacle.

Maintaining stability amid movement

Effective principals understand that movement and disruption are essential, but they also recognize the importance of maintaining stability in certain areas. Like tectonic plates that stabilize the land even as they shift, principals provide a steady foundation of support and consistency. For instance, while pushing for instructional innovation, the principal ensures the school's core values remain unchanged, offering the community a sense of continuity and reassurance. This balance prevents the change process from feeling overwhelming and builds trust in the principal's leadership.

> This leadership approach is not about causing chaos but about making room for something better and reshaping the educational experience to reflect equity, innovation, and success. The principal becomes a catalyst for transformation, leaving behind a legacy of leadership that may move mountains—one thoughtful shift at a time.

Recognizing blind spots

Overloading the fault lines
There is risk in applying too much pressure too quickly, overloading the system and causing unnecessary upheaval. Like tectonic plates that shift too abruptly and trigger earthquakes, a principal who pushes too hard for immediate change may destabilize the school community. Gradual movement, paired with clear communication about the rationale and timeline for each change, minimizes the risk of overwhelming the school's capacity for transformation.

Neglecting the unseen layers
It's important to consider the unseen layers of the school's culture—deep-seated beliefs, traditions, and emotions that may not be immediately visible but strongly influence how change is received. Like tectonic plates that are affected by the layers of rock and magma beneath them, a principal's initiatives can be shaped by underlying dynamics like mistrust, fear of failure, or a history of failed initiatives. Listening to concerns and acknowledging the perspectives of the school community creates a foundation of trust that can support sustainable change.

Friction without resolution
Friction is inevitable in tectonic leadership, but unresolved tension can create ongoing conflict that erodes morale and trust. A principal who challenges the status quo without offering clear pathways for resolution risks alienating those who feel disoriented or unsupported by the change process. For instance, a principal who criticizes outdated teaching methods without providing professional development or resources leaves teachers feeling attacked rather than empowered. Principals should give staff the tools, training, and encouragement to navigate the shifts successfully. Acknowledging the challenges and celebrating incremental progress ensures that friction becomes a catalyst for growth rather than a source of division.

The goal of tectonic leadership is to make thoughtful, sustainable, and inclusive progress. By balancing pressure with support, vision with empathy, and disruption with stability, principals can guide their schools toward transformation while preserving the community's trust and cohesion.

Reflective prompts

Cracking the surface
- Am I focusing on areas where movement will create the most significant impact?
- Am I aware of the areas in my school community already experiencing stress or strain?

Knowing where the pressure is building allows principals to avoid exacerbating existing challenges and to prioritize their efforts effectively.

Balancing the pressure
- Am I applying just enough pressure to provoke change without overwhelming the school community?
- Am I creating opportunities for minor adjustments before introducing more significant shifts?

Gradual, incremental changes can often make the overall transformation more accessible and less intimidating for the community.

Riding the tectonic friction
- How am I responding to resistance when it arises?
- Am I communicating the purpose of the friction as part of the growth process?

Resistance often signals that people are processing change. Clear communication about why tension exists can help transform it into collaboration.

Reconfiguring the landscape
- Am I considering how changes in one area might affect other parts of the school ecosystem?
- Am I seeking input from diverse stakeholders to understand potential ripple effects?

Broad perspectives can help the principal identify unintended consequences and address them proactively.

> Tectonic leadership requires principals to be both deliberate and reflective in their actions. When approached with care and intentionality, the shifts they create can transform the educational landscape into one where growth and innovation thrive.

Summary

Tectonic leadership embodies the art of deliberate disruption and intentional progress. It recognizes that true transformation requires movement—sometimes slow and steady, sometimes intense and uncomfortable—but always purposeful. For principals, this approach means embracing their role as a catalyst for change, knowing that meaningful shifts often begin with unsettling the status quo.

This leadership is not without its challenges. Moving the right "plates" requires a deep understanding of the forces at play: the cultural dynamics, systemic inequities, and entrenched habits that may resist change. Principals must navigate these forces carefully, applying just enough pressure to provoke progress without causing irreparable disruption. They must also anticipate and address the inevitable friction, reframing resistance as an opportunity for dialogue and collaboration rather than a roadblock. Through transparent communication, empathy, and support, they turn tension into energy for collective growth.

Chapter 39

The WAIT principle: Why am I talking?

In a dynamic and multifaceted leadership role like that of a school principal, the ability to listen deeply is one of the most critical skills for fostering trust, understanding, and collaboration within the school community. The WAIT principle—standing for "Why am I talking?"—is a helpful reminder for principals to be intentional about when they speak and when they listen. It emphasizes the importance of creating space for others to share their thoughts, experiences, and ideas without the principal dominating the conversation.

For principals, listening is not a passive act; it's a powerful tool for building trust and strengthening relationships. When principals ask themselves, "Why am I talking?" and shift their focus to understanding others, they demonstrate that they value the perspectives, experiences, and voices of their teachers, students, and parents. This intentional act of listening lays the foundation for trust, showing the school community that the principal is genuinely interested in hearing what they have to say.

The WAIT principle encourages principals to be strategic about speaking, ensuring that when they do contribute, it is purposeful and adds value to the conversation. By prioritizing listening first, principals gather more accurate and comprehensive information, leading to better decision-making.

The WAIT principle is also a valuable tool for managing emotions and responses in challenging situations. In a high-pressure role like a principal's, there are times when stress, frustration, or urgency can lead to quick reactions rather than thoughtful responses. By pausing to ask, "Why am I talking?" principals create a moment of reflection, allowing them to consider whether their contribution will add value or if it's better to continue listening. This pause can prevent emotionally driven or reactive responses that might escalate a situation or inadvertently close down dialogue.

The WAIT principle is a reminder that effective leadership begins with deep listening. By focusing on understanding before speaking, principals build trust, encourage inclusivity, make better decisions, and model reflective practice. This approach strengthens relationships within the school community, empowers others to take on leadership roles, and contributes meaningfully to the school's development.

What this looks like

Facilitating conversations, not controlling them

School leaders who practise the WAIT principle view their role as a facilitator rather than the dominant voice in meetings and discussions. They consciously step back, allowing others to share their perspectives and insights before contributing their own thoughts. This approach encourages a more inclusive conversation and helps uncover ideas or concerns that might not surface if the principal speaks too soon or too often. When the principal does speak, their comments are often more informed, thoughtful, and directly relevant to what others have shared.

Asking questions to empower problem-solving

A principal who practises the WAIT principle knows that their role is not always to provide answers but to ask the right questions that stimulate reflection and deeper understanding. For instance, when a teacher approaches the principal with a classroom challenge, instead of immediately offering advice, the principal might ask, "What do you think are the key factors contributing to this situation?" or "How have you addressed similar issues in the past?" These questions encourage the teacher to explore the situation more deeply and identify potential strategies. By prioritizing questions over directives, the principal supports a culture of self-reflection and collaborative problem-solving.

Actively listening in difficult conversations
The WAIT principle is especially important during challenging or emotionally charged conversations. A principal who embraces the WAIT principle listens attentively, acknowledging the other person's emotions and concerns. They refrain from interrupting, avoid rushing to conclusions, and ensure that they fully understand the issue. Only after fully hearing the other's perspective does the principal offer their response or explain the rationale behind the decision. This patient and empathetic approach demonstrates that the principal values input, even if they ultimately disagree, and fosters a more respectful and constructive conversation.

Practising silence as a leadership tool
Silence can be a powerful tool in leadership, yet it is often underused. Whether it's pausing to let someone finish their thought, giving space for a moment of reflection, or allowing others to fill the silence with their insights, the principal uses silence to create a more thoughtful and deliberate dialogue. This pause signals genuine interest in hearing from others and not rushing to offer an opinion. The strategic use of silence encourages deeper reflection and ensures the conversation is not driven solely by the principal's perspective.

> The WAIT principle transforms a principal's leadership from one of authority to one of deep engagement, active listening, and thoughtful communication. Principals who follow it understand that sometimes the most influential leadership involves saying less and listening more.

Recognizing blind spots

Mistaking silence for genuine listening
The WAIT principle is is sometimes misinterpreted to mean that simply speaking less equates to effective listening. A principal might fall into the trap of remaining silent during discussions, assuming their silence alone means they are listening well. However, genuine listening involves active

engagement, asking clarifying questions, and reflecting on what is being said—not merely withholding comments.

Being perceived as passive or indecisive

While it's essential to create space for others to share, there are times when a principal's voice is needed to provide direction, clarity, or a final decision. If the principal is overly focused on waiting to speak, they may miss opportunities to assert leadership, especially when decisiveness or clear guidance is called for. Principals must balance creating space for others with confidently stepping in when leadership is needed.

Allowing dominant voices to overshadow quieter perspectives

Giving space for others to speak sometimes risks the dominant voices monopolizing the conversation. The principal needs to know when to step in to ensure dialogue is inclusive and all voices are heard. They can lead by inviting quieter participants to share, posing direct questions to a range of individuals, and encouraging diverse perspectives.

Overlooking nonverbal communication

Listening involves paying attention to both what is said verbally and what is communicated through body language, tone of voice, and facial expressions. A principal who focuses too much on verbal listening might miss important nonverbal cues that provide additional context or reveal underlying emotions. Principals should cultivate the habit of reading nonverbal signals, checking in with individuals to ensure they fully understand the context, and acknowledging verbal and nonverbal feedback in their responses.

> The WAIT approach to leadership helps build a school environment where all voices are valued, conflicts are addressed constructively, and decisions are made with a comprehensive understanding of the needs and perspectives of the entire community.

Reflective prompts

Am I listening or simply waiting to speak?
- When engaging in conversations, do I genuinely focus on understanding the other person's perspective, or am I formulating my response while they are speaking?
- How often do I intentionally create opportunities for quieter individuals to share their perspectives?

Principals can evaluate the authenticity of their engagement by considering whether they are truly listening to understand or simply waiting to reply.

Am I reacting or responding thoughtfully?
- In emotionally charged situations, do I pause to consider the impact of my words before speaking?
- Am I able to remain composed and present during difficult conversations, showing that I value the other person's input?

Leadership often involves navigating sensitive or contentious issues, and the ability to pause before responding can prevent misunderstandings and build trust.

Am I encouraging collaboration or stifling it?
- Do I ask open-ended questions that invite deeper reflection and dialogue, or do my questions tend to be leading or close-ended, limiting the conversation?
- How often do I follow up on what others have shared, demonstrating that I value their input and am willing to incorporate their ideas into decision-making?

Effective listening also means fostering collaboration. Principals should consider whether their actions and questions encourage meaningful dialogue or unintentionally limit it.

Am I balancing listening and leadership?
- Do I know when to step in to provide clarity or guidance without overshadowing the contributions of others?
- How do I ensure my leadership is perceived as confident and decisive while still prioritizing inclusivity and collaboration?

While listening is essential, effective leadership also requires knowing when to provide direction. Reflecting on this balance ensures the principal maintains authority while fostering a culture of respect and inclusion.

> By consistently asking these reflective questions, principals ensure they embody the WAIT principle in a way that strengthens their leadership and fosters a positive school culture. This approach balances listening with decisive action, empowering the entire school community to contribute to meaningful conversations and collective decision-making. The result is a more collaborative, trusting, and inclusive school environment where every voice matters.

Summary

Principals who embrace the WAIT principle understand that leadership is not always about having the right answers or dominating every discussion. Effective leadership is about facilitating dialogue, empowering others, and building a culture where everyone feels heard and valued. By intentionally asking, "Why am I talking?" principals create space for the ideas, insights, and concerns of teachers, students, and parents to surface, leading to richer conversations, more informed decision-making, and a greater sense of shared ownership within the school community.

When time is limited, and the pressure to make quick decisions is high, the WAIT principle is a reminder that sometimes the most powerful thing a principal can do is listen. When practised consistently and thoughtfully, the WAIT principle transforms leadership into a meaningful dialogue, laying the foundation for a more connected, resilient, and flourishing school community.

Chapter 40

Lunar leadership: Gentle influence, powerful impact

In school leadership, a principal's authority is a resource that, when used thoughtfully, can inspire meaningful change without exerting overt control. Like the moon's gravitational pull on the earth, which shapes tides with quiet force, a principal's influence can have a profound impact when applied with subtlety and respect. Research shows that influence, built on trust and collaboration, is far more effective and enduring than authority alone. Principals who lead with this steady force inspire commitment, foster shared purpose, and create a culture of respect and cooperation.

Leading with influence also requires a commitment to equity and inclusivity. Principals must ensure that all voices, primarily those historically marginalized, are heard and valued. Creating opportunities for open dialogue, amplifying diverse perspectives, and addressing systemic barriers strengthen collaboration and ensure that every school community member feels empowered.

Experts James Kouzes and Barry Posner emphasize that leadership rooted in empathy and respect has a more lasting impact than authority-driven directives. People are more motivated and engaged when their voices matter and their contributions are valued. For example, a principal who involves teachers in problem-solving or invites staff input during decision-making demonstrates this influence, creating a "gravitational pull" that fosters collective ownership and progress.

Like the moon's pull shapes tides without disrupting balance, principals must guide without overshadowing. Balancing authority and influence involves empowering staff while steering the school toward shared goals. For instance, in a crisis, a principal may need to act decisively for safety, but in daily operations, they might encourage staff autonomy and innovation. This balance fosters trust, creativity, and resilience.

Challenges like resistance to change or competing priorities can test this balance. In such moments, influence and authority must work together—offering firm guidance while maintaining trust and collaboration. By navigating these complexities with empathy and intention, principals reinforce their credibility and strengthen their school's collective resolve.

Influence is not passive; it demands deliberate action. Principals can lead by facilitating shared decision-making, practising active listening, and celebrating contributions. For example, publicly recognizing staff achievements or encouraging teacher-led initiatives reinforces a sense of ownership and pride. These practices ensure that influence remains a practical force, shaping the school's culture daily.

What this looks like

Empowering staff through subtle support

Much like the moon's gravitational pull that allows the tides to rise and fall naturally, a principal who leads with gentle influence supports staff autonomy while providing subtle guidance. They empower teachers to lead within their classrooms, make decisions about curriculum, and take ownership of their professional growth. Rather than enforcing rigid deadlines or stringent reporting, they create structures that promote self-reflection and encourage growth. This type of accountability helps each person stay aligned with the school's goals without exerting pressure, allowing progress to emerge naturally and sustainably.

Respecting each person's unique gravity

A principal leading with gentle influence respects the individuality of each teacher, student, and staff member. They recognize that each person brings unique strengths and perspectives that are essential to the school's success. This approach reinforces a culture where everyone's contributions are seen as valuable, creating a school environment of mutual respect and appreciation.

Maintaining a consistent, quiet presence

The moon's pull is unwavering and predictable, creating stability in the natural world. Similarly, a principal who leads through gentle influence provides consistent, quiet guidance that staff and students can rely on. This presence is reassuring, showing the school community that the principal can always offer support and guidance without micromanaging. Their steady presence cultivates trust, allowing the school to evolve in an environment of security and continuity.

> Just as the moon's gravitational pull shapes the tides and ecosystems even when it cannot be seen, a principal's quiet influence can transform a school's culture, guiding it toward a future marked by shared vision, mutual respect, and lasting positive change.

Recognizing blind spots

Risk of losing impact: When influence feels too subtle

The moon's pull shapes the tides, but that influence is not always immediately noticeable. Similarly, a principal's gentle influence may not be noticed if it is too subtle or indirect, and therefore risks losing impact. Staff and students may misunderstand or overlook the principal's intentions, assuming that the lack of direct instruction indicates a lack of urgency or priority. Confusion or inconsistency may result if individuals interpret the principal's direction differently.

Misinterpreting silence as agreement: Assuming quiet means consent

A principal who leads with subtlety may interpret staff and student silence as acceptance of their ideas, only to discover later that there are unvoiced concerns, misunderstandings, or resistance beneath the surface. The blind spot of misinterpreting silence can result in stalled initiatives or missed opportunities for improvement.

Over-focusing on influence: Struggling to establish authority

Principals who focus heavily on influence may struggle to assert authority when needed. There are moments when decisiveness is required, especially in times of conflict or crisis, and a principal who relies solely on influence may be seen as indecisive or overly passive. This can weaken their ability to lead effectively when immediate action is necessary.

A principal who understands the nuances of gentle influence leads with a steady, guiding presence—empowering others while maintaining a quiet yet powerful pull that can inspire lasting, positive transformation.

Reflective prompts

Balancing subtlety with decisiveness

- Do I recognize when to shift from gentle influence to decisive action?
- Am I prepared to provide clear direction or feedback when a more authoritative approach is needed?

Principals should know when gentle guidance is practical and when more substantial authority is needed.

Phases of the moon: Adaptability

- Does my leadership style reflect the moon's gentle pull, or is it causing high tides and turbulence?
- Am I flexible in my leadership to meet the evolving needs of my school?

The moon's phases symbolize change and adaptability. Principals should reflect on how their leadership style shapes the school's atmosphere.

Honouring individual gravity

- Am I respecting each staff member's unique expertise and allowing them to make decisions independently?
- Do I offer gentle support and guidance when needed, or am I creating too much autonomy that leads to isolation or inconsistency?

CHAPTER 40

Like the moon's pull that influences every ocean differently while maintaining a global rhythm, principals should empower individuals while ensuring the entire school remains cohesive and unified.

Exercising influence thoughtfully and effectively can help foster a supportive and collaborative school environment. A principal's influence should be steady, nurturing, and empowering.

Summary

The metaphor of the moon's subtle and constant influence captures the essence of a principal's leadership when it is rooted in gentle guidance. A principal who leads in this way understands that leadership is not always about commanding attention but about creating an atmosphere where others feel empowered to grow and contribute. This leader respects the strengths and individuality of each person, valuing collaboration over control and influence over command. They recognize their school community's collective power, and that progress emerges when each member feels valued and invested in the school's vision. The moon's quiet pull symbolizes their leadership philosophy—one that shapes without forcing and uplifts without overpowering.

Leading with gentle influence is an invitation to lead with humility, patience, and vision. It is about guiding the school's journey steadily, knowing that the most impactful transformations often happen gradually and with care. A leader who embraces this approach harnesses the quiet power of their position to create a school culture that is resilient, cohesive, and ready to take on each new challenge and opportunity with confidence.

Conclusion

Leadership is inherently complex—messy, unpredictable, and deeply personal. Through the metaphors and lessons shared in this book, I hope you've gained a clearer understanding of what it means to lead as a principal. Your influence may sometimes be unseen, but it is profoundly felt. Effective leadership is not about adhering to a strict set of rules; it's about adapting, responding, and growing in step with your students, staff, and community. Leadership, like learning, is a dynamic, lifelong process.

As you reflect on the journey now that you've completed *A Year of Leading*, I invite you to take a moment to acknowledge the ground you've covered through some of those complexities. And as you continue your leadership journey, remember that there will be moments of doubt when you feel overwhelmed or unsure of the path ahead. These moments are natural, and they are part of the growth process. When they arise, I encourage you to pause, breathe, and reconnect with the core principles explored in this book. Effective leaders don't always have the right answers, but they are willing to stay present, reflect, and find the courage to make the next best decision, even when the way forward isn't entirely clear.

This leadership journey shouldn't be taken alone. Along the way, you will continue to learn from those around you: your colleagues, your mentors, your students. You'll even learn from your missteps! Let those experiences shape and inform your leadership. Be open to feedback, be willing to ask for help, and know that vulnerability is not a weakness but a strength. It allows others to see you as human and creates a genuine connection.

As you navigate the complexity of school leadership, I hope you'll also find moments of joy—whether it's the quiet satisfaction of watching a student succeed, the camaraderie of a supportive team, or the beauty of a community coming together to face a challenge. These moments will remind you why this work matters and will fuel your determination to keep going.

Think back to my story in the Introduction of young Grace's simple yet profound question to me: "What do you do?" The answer is that you lead, and at its heart, leadership helps others thrive. As a leader, you help your staff, your students, and your community find their paths to success. You create an environment where everyone feels valued, supported, and capable of doing their best work. Your role is to nurture that potential, to guide and inspire, and to trust that the small, everyday actions you take add up to something much more significant.

A Year of Leading has been designed to guide you, help you reflect, and offer insight, but ultimately, your wisdom and experience will shape your leadership in the years to come. As you step forward, embrace the truth that leadership is never about reaching a final destination—it is about continually showing up, learning, and evolving. Some days will feel effortless, while others will test your patience, resilience, and resolve. But in every moment, in every conversation, in every challenge, you have the opportunity to lead with clarity, compassion, and conviction. Trust yourself. Trust the relationships you've nurtured. Trust that even when the path ahead is uncertain, your presence, your courage, and your commitment make a difference.

Thank you for choosing to lead with intention. Thank you for being the kind of leader who listens, who learns, who shows up even when the work is hard. Schools thrive because of leaders like you—those who believe in the power of community, who recognize that leadership is not about perfection but about purpose. It has been an honour to walk this journey with you through *A Year of Leading*, and I hope you will carry its lessons forward, not as a rigid roadmap, but as a companion to your own wisdom and experience.

So take a breath. Take a step. And keep leading with heart. You are exactly where you need to be.

References

Aguilar, E. (2016). *The art of coaching teams: Building resilient communities that transform schools.* Jossey-Bass.

Avolio, B. J., & Gardner, W. L. (2005). Authentic leadership development: Getting to the root of positive forms of leadership. *The Leadership Quarterly, 16*(3), 315–338.

Berkovich, I., & Eyal, O. (2020). An examination of the emotional intelligence of school principals and the impact on school climate in public schools in the United Arab Emirates. *Journal of Educational Administration.*

Brown, B. (2012). *Daring greatly: How the courage to be vulnerable transforms the way we live, love, parent, and lead.* Gotham Books.

Cameron, K., & Spreitzer, G. (2012). *The Oxford handbook of positive organizational scholarship.* Oxford University Press.

Collins, J. (2001). *Good to great: Why some companies make the leap… and others don't.* HarperBusiness.

Covey, S. R. (1989). *The 7 habits of highly effective people: Powerful lessons in personal change.* Simon & Schuster.

Drucker, P. F. (2008). *Management* (Rev. ed.). HarperCollins.

DuFour, R., DuFour, R., Eaker, R., & Many, T. (2010). *Learning by Doing: A handbook for professional learning communities at work.* Solution Tree Press.

Emmons, R. A., & McCullough, M. E. (2003). Counting blessings versus burdens: An experimental investigation of gratitude and subjective well-being in daily life. *Journal of Personality and Social Psychology,* 84(2), 377–389. https://doi.org/10.1037/0022-3514.84.2.377

Frankl, V. E. (2006). *Man's search for meaning.* Beacon Press. (Original work published 1946)

Fullan, M. (2001). *Leading in a culture of change.* Jossey-Bass.

Fullan, M. (2014). *The principal: Three keys to maximizing impact.* Jossey-Bass.

Goleman, D. (1995). *Emotional intelligence: Why it can matter more than IQ.* Bantam Books.

Goleman, D. (2000). Leadership that gets results. *Harvard Business Review,* 78(2), 78–90.

Goleman, D., Boyatzis, R., & McKee, A. (2002). *Primal leadership: Realizing the power of emotional intelligence.* Harvard Business Review Press.

Harms, P. D., Credé, M., Tynan, M., Leon, M., & Jeung, W. (2017). Leadership and stress: A meta-analytic review. *Journal of Applied Psychology,* 102(12), 1866–1884.

Heifetz, R. A., Grashow, A., & Linsky, M. (2009). *The practice of adaptive leadership: Tools and tactics for changing your organization and the world.* Harvard Business Press.

Kidder, R. M. (1995). *How good people make tough choices: Resolving the dilemmas of ethical living.* HarperCollins.

Kotter, J. P. (1996). *Leading change.* Harvard Business School Press.

Kouzes, J. M., & Posner, B. Z. (2017). *The leadership challenge: How to make extraordinary things happen in organizations.* Jossey-Bass.

Leithwood, K., & Riehl, C. (2005). *What we know about successful school leadership.* Laboratory for Student Success at Temple University.

Lencioni, P. M. (2002). *The five dysfunctions of a team: A leadership fable.* Jossey-Bass.

Lipsky, D., & Seeber, R. (2006). *Managing organizational conflict.* Jossey-Bass.

Mullen, C. A., & Rhodes, M. (2007). *Principals in peril: The self-defeating characteristics of leadership that drive school failure.* Palgrave Macmillan.

Robinson, V. M. J. (2008). Forging the links between distributed leadership and educational outcomes. *Journal of Educational Administration, 46*(2), 241–256.

Robinson, V. M. J. (2011). *Student-centered leadership.* Jossey-Bass.

Scharmer, C. O. (2009). *Theory U: Leading from the future as it emerges.* Berrett-Koehler.

Schein, E. H. (2010). *Organizational culture and leadership.* Jossey-Bass.

Seligman, M. E. P. (2011). *Flourish: A visionary new understanding of happiness and well-being.* Atria Books.

Senge, P. M. (1990). *The fifth discipline: The art and practice of the learning organization.* Doubleday.

Sergiovanni, T. J. (1996). *Leadership for the schoolhouse: How is it different? Why is it important?* Jossey-Bass.

Spillane, J. P., Halverson, R., & Diamond, J. B. (2004). Towards a theory of leadership practice: A distributed perspective. *Teachers College Record, 105*(3), 424–451.

Sutton, R. I. (2007). *The no asshole rule: Building a civilized workplace and surviving one that isn't.* Business Plus.

Tschannen-Moran, M. (2004). *Trust matters: Leadership for successful schools.* Jossey-Bass.

Wang, F. (2018). Subversive leadership and power tactics. *Journal of Educational Administration, 56*(4), 398–413. https://doi.org/10.1108/JEA-07-2017-0081

Wheatley, M. J. (2006). *Leadership and the new science: Discovering order in a chaotic world.* Berrett-Koehler Publishers.

About the Author

Kevin Reimer is a leader, educator, and coach with over 30 years of experience advancing school leadership and fostering positive educational change. In 2013, The Learning Partnership honoured Kevin as one of Canada's Outstanding Principals, a testament to his impactful contributions to the field.

Kevin's career is defined by his unwavering commitment to supporting educational leaders and creating environments where students, teachers, and school communities thrive. As the President and Executive Director of the British Columbia Principals' and Vice-Principals' Association, Kevin championed the professional growth and well-being of school leaders across the province. His collaboration with the Ministry of Education resulted in developing a leadership platform that serves as a cornerstone for principal and vice-principal development. It equips aspiring and current school leaders with the tools, strategies, and confidence needed to meet the demands of an ever-evolving educational landscape. Other work with the Ministry of Education and the provincial government was instrumental in establishing a mentoring program and advancing equitable employment practices for principals and vice-principals. These initiatives have left a lasting legacy on the landscape of educational leadership in British Columbia.

Known for his innovative approach to collaboration, Kevin has designed district-wide structures that encourage teamwork, transparency, and a shared commitment to excellence. His efforts to build positive school cultures have empowered educators and inspired student success, reinforcing his belief in the transformative power of strong leadership.

Now an International Coaching Federation–certified coach, Kevin focuses on empowering leaders to navigate complex challenges with clarity and resilience. Through his coaching practice, he helps clients uncover their potential, embrace reflective practices, and lead with purpose and authenticity. His unique perspective is informed by years of visiting schools, engaging with principals, and understanding the nuances of leadership across diverse contexts.

www.ingramcontent.com/pod-product-compliance
Lightning Source LLC
Chambersburg PA
CBHW020340010526
44119CB00048B/534